ECONOMIC WELFARE

AND THE DEVELOPMENT OF

THE MOHAWK REGION

ECONOMIC WELFARE

AND THE DEVELOPMENT OF

THE MOHAWK REGION

Richard J. Kalish and Donald J. Reeb

Assistant Professors of Political Economy
Graduate School of Public Affairs
State University of New York at Albany

GRADUATE SCHOOL OF PUBLIC AFFAIRS
STATE UNIVERSITY OF NEW YORK AT ALBANY
ALBANY, NEW YORK

HC
107
.N7
.K34

Printed in the United States of America
by Williams Press, Incorporated, Albany, New York

Foreword

The Graduate School of Public Affairs was established in 1962 by State University of New York to provide educational preparation for academic and public service careers, assist in the continuing professional development of government executives, and undertake research on significant public problems and issues. To make generally available such research by its faculty members, the Graduate School established a monograph series on public policy issues. This monograph is the sixth in the series.

Lewis P. Welch
Acting Dean

Preface

The origin of this monograph is traceable to a contract with the New York State Office of Planning Coordination for a study of the economy of the Mohawk Region—Fulton, Hamilton, Herkimer, Lewis, Montgomery, and Oneida Counties.

The authors are indebted to several colleagues at the Graduate School of Public Affairs of the State University of New York at Albany. Professors Orville F. Poland and Jack E. Gelfand provided the impetus to undertake the study and Professor Melvin Bers listened to our worries and provided much counseling during the study. The research divisions of a large number of New York State Departments provided valuable assistance in the collection of data and we wish to acknowledge their aid and advice.

Last and certainly not least, we wish to express our deep thanks to our assistants: John Finn, Donald Swire, Helen Aicher, and Mary Williams. Professor Joseph F. Zimmerman and Mrs. Judith B. Lickona provided expert editorial advice as well as supervision of the publication of this monograph.

Table of Contents

List of Tables

List of Charts and Graphs

List of Maps

CHAPTER 1

Regional Income and Development

The subject of this study is a six-county region—Fulton, Hamilton, Herkimer, Lewis, Montgomery, and Oneida—in Upstate New York. The period of study is 1940-1964, with adjustments for availability of data. The six-county region—the Mohawk Region—has not fared well relative to national income increases. In 1948, the per capita income in the Region was five dollars below that of the nation; in 1964 the difference had increased to $311. Table A-1 indicates the increasing differential in per capita income which is the empirical focus for this study. The monograph attempts to answer the question: "Why did the income and development of the Region lag relative to that of the nation and other regions?"

Regional Income

An economic study which uses regional income as the focus requires some defense. The reasons for studying regional income and making it central in a regional economic analysis are several.

First, regional income indicates the level of output and the sum total of regional incomes equals national income. The latter equals the value added to all goods and services produced.

Second, income indicates the amount that all individuals can claim in currently produced products and services.

Third, income is a measure of economic welfare which enters most discussions of regional objective functions.

Fourth, income when divided by inputs such as employment indicates economic efficiency. If the supply of inputs is fixed, increases

1

Table A-1

Per Capita Personal Income [1]
1964-1948*

| | Per Capita Income | | | Growth Rate (Per Cent) | |
	1948	1964	Absolute Change	Mean	Standard Deviation
Nation	$1901	$2518	$617	2.1	1.2
New York	2407	3103	696	1.6	1.1
Upstate	1997	2423	426	1.2	1.4
Region	1896	2207	311	1.0	1.0

[1] The data are in constant dollars, 1963=100.0, using the GNP deflator index. Upstate refers to New York State less the nine New York counties in the New York Standard Metropolitan Statistical Area.

* New York State Department of Commerce, *Personal Income in Counties of New York State 1964*, (Albany: 1966), pp. 16-17; *Survey of Current Business*, April, 1966, p. 11.

in economic activity depend entirely upon increasing the economic efficiency in the use of each input.[1]

The above reasons are not sufficient for government interest in regional income. It need be added that there is evidence that the present market and governmentally institutionalized forces are insufficient to provide maximum efficiency in use of scarce resources; *e.g.*, there is serious unemployment in several regions of the United States and there is a large amount of disguised unemployment in several industries. Insofar as either or both of these conditions exist in a region, its per capita income will be lower, *ceteris paribus*. A regional income policy is a fit object for government concern because an improvement in the efficiency of resource use in one region could be of benefit to the entire nation.

The perspective here is regional per capita income in the nation. A somewhat narrower and more provincial attitude would be re-

---

[1] Edgar M. Hoover and Joseph L. Fisher, "Research in Regional Economic Growth", *Problems in the Study of Economic Growth* (New York: National Bureau of Economic Research, 1949), pp. 173-250; and Werner Z. Hirsch, "A General Structure for Regional Economic Analysis", in Werner Hochwald (ed.), *Design of Regional Accounts* (Baltimore: The Johns Hopkins Press, 1961), pp. 4-13.

gional per capita income increases with no necessary change in national per capita income. Such a perspective is possible and it is possible that a case could be made for the occurrence of regional per capita income increases through the transference of incomes from other regions. The argument for a gain in regional per capita income at the expense of some other region must necessarily involve some theory of geography; *e.g.,* a system of cities hypothesis and policy, but this would be far beyond the focus of this study. Of course, production and employment do transfer from one region to another without any equilibrating market forces to realign regional per capita incomes such that they remain equal or proportionate, but this does more to indicate the focus for policy and analysis than it alters the perspective of this study. More precisely, recognition that production transfers between regions can change the level of regional per capita income requires that the central question of this study be altered to: "Does the increasing per capita income differential between the Mohawk Region and the nation reflect decreasing efficiency in resource use in the Region or other factors?"

To form the question thusly is to include implicitly a host of variables and these need be considered explicity for the analysis. Some of these variables are usually termed demographic; *e.g.,* ethnicity, population size, age structure of population, education, school enrollments, and employment population ratios. Other variables are usually termed economic; *e.g.,* employment, unemployment, income by type and source, productivity, rate of return on investment, mix of industry, commutation, and migration. The dividing line between economic and demographic variables is not clear—the usual philosophical problem of classification rears its ugly head—but the inclusion of these variables under the one rubric or the other is hardly to be questioned.

That the demographic variables can affect the registered level of per capita income in a region is easily shown in a hypothetical example.

Per capita regional income is lower in Region A because of a lower employment/population ratio—forty per cent—than that in Region B where the ratio is fifty per cent; all other parts of income per capita in the two regions are in proportion to each other. Region A is ten per cent of Region B in terms of employment in each in-

	REGION A	REGION B
Industry I	$1000	$10,000
Industry II	2000	20,000
Total Income (Y)	$3000	$30,000
Employment (N)	10	100
Y/N	$ 300	$ 300
Population (P)	25	200
Y/P	$ 120	$ 150

dustry, total income, and total employment and is identical in income per employee. The differential in employment/population ratios could be the result of Region A having a larger portion of its population in school, unemployed, retired, non-working women, institutionalized, and/or unable to work because of sickness or discrimination. Some of these conditions can be changed. Which ones the society chooses to change and the methods to be used in the programs must depend on the policy decisions in our federal system of governments; *e.g.,* the national government requires that discrimination be eliminated and the state governments choose to require school attendance until age sixteen. The local governments can choose to either accept these standards or to increase their stringency but not to ignore the minima imposed by the federal and state governments. Analysis can describe the existing conditions; public decisions publicly made must be the source for the policies.

The variables under the rubric economic also can be shown to affect the registered per capita income in a region. If Industry I

	REGION A		REGION B	
	Employment	Total Wages	Employment	Total Wages
Industry I ($10,000 per employee)	1000	$10,000,000	2000	$20,000,000
Industry II ($5,000 per employee)	2000	10,000,000	1000	5,000,000
	3000	$20,000,000	3000	$25,000,000
Average Wage		$ 6,666		$ 8,333

pays twice the wages per employee that Industry II pays—*e.g.,* $10,000 per year per employee *vs.* $5,000 per year per employee—

then income per employee in Region A will be $6,666 and in Region B $8,333. The result obtains because of differences in industry *mix*, not from any differences in demography. In this example it is assumed that pay per employee in the same industry is the same—all employees in Industry I receive the same wage whether they work in Region A or B. Differentials in wages per employee can exist along with and independent of differentials in employment mix.

Definitionally, the wages received per employee are equal to the following:

$$W = \frac{SQ}{N} \quad \text{where} \quad \begin{aligned} W &= \text{wage per employee} \\ N &= \text{employees} \\ S &= \text{prices of production} \\ Q &= \text{quantity of production} \end{aligned}$$

The numerator, SQ, could be defined as total revenue. However, since part of total revenue includes the prices of intermediary products such as raw materials, SQ will be defined as equal to value added, or the quantity of the production which these employees added to the output times the price of this increment. Included in value added is a payment to ownership; *i.e.,* profit, which is ignored for the present.

Since W—the wage rate—depends on a ratio between value added and employees, and value added itself depends on prices and quantities, then any factor which raises S or Q or lowers N will, *ceteris paribus,* raise the wage rate. That is, the differentials in wage rates in the same industry can be the result of differentials in S, Q, or N. Differentials in each of these can exist for a variety of reasons: S may be higher than the all-industry average because of advantageous transportation costs, monopolistic market conditions, advertising, or other deviations from perfect competition; Q may be higher because of lower input costs, better methods of production, more efficient management, or other such factors; N may be lower because of a lack of in-migration, or any of the other factors which were discussed under demography.

The element in SQ which was ignored is gross proprietor's income (GPI) which is the return to ownership for invested capital. More precisely, then, the equation for wages is a ratio with SQ-GPI in the numerator and N in the denominator. Thus, if SQ rises by a greater absolute amount than does GPI while N is constant, then W must increase.

In sum, per capita income in a region is the result of various elements. On the economic side of the equation, per capita income is affected by the wages received in each regional industry, employment in each regional industry, profits, and other factors; and on the demographic side, by population characteristics. An illustrative equation of these elements is shown below, where the W's refer to wage rates,

$$\frac{Y}{P} = \frac{(W_1)(N_1) + (W_2)(N_2) + \ldots + (W_n)(N_n) + Z_1 + \ldots + Z_n}{P_A + P_B + \ldots + P_N}$$

the N's to employment, the P's to population characteristics, and the Z's to non-wage income. A region's per capita income differential is seen to be the result of a host of factors. Only by careful analysis and disaggregation can the sources of a region's per capita income differential be uncovered.

Definitions

There are several statistical sources for regional income data. The definitions used in this chapter, and for most of the analysis, are those used by the United States and New York State Departments of Commerce. The concept is personal income—the current income received by *residents* of a region before deductions for direct personal income taxes, but after deductions for individuals' contributions to social security, governmental retirement, and other social insurance programs. Personal income includes: (a) wages and salaries: private and government allocations for services rendered, including tips, commissions, payments-in-kind, but not employers' contributions to social insurance programs; (b) proprietors' income: net business earnings of owners of unincorporated enterprises including farms; (c) property income: rental income, the imputed rent of owner-occupied dwellings, dividends, interest, and other property earnings; (d) other income: individual receipts for injuries, old age and survivors benefits, unemployment insurance receipts, relief, military pensions, payments by business for other than current participation in production, and the net difference between current contributions by employers to insurance and pension plans and the current contributions by employees and the self-employed to these programs.[2]

The first two types of income—wages and salaries plus proprietors' income are referred to as *participation income*. When the third type of income—property income—is added to participation income, the three class combination is referred to as *production income*. Participation income is, for the most part, received for direct or personal service participation in the current production of goods and services, while production income includes payment for personal services and payment for capital or savings use.

Regional population is defined as the total number of residents of the region. This includes the population not in institutions plus the persons in institutions in the state assigned to the counties in which they lived before entering the institution. This definition of population is used to compute per capita income. An alternative definition that is used in the United States Census of Population tabulates the institutional population as residing in the region in which the institution is located. The latter definition of population is used in the demographic analysis.

Regional employment is defined either as the number of persons employed in plants located in the region or the number of persons residing in a region who also are employed. The totals are equal if there is zero net commutation. While much of the employment analysis uses the latter concept—employment of residents—the empirical analysis of productivity and other economic characteristics of employers uses the first concept of regional employment.

Regional distribution of income is measured by use of either a Gini index or an interdecile index. The latter is the income received by the ninetieth per cent family or other population unit minus the income received by the tenth per cent family divided by the sum of the same two figures. If all family incomes are equal, the value of the index is 0.00. The Gini index also has the limits of zero and one—an equal income received by each family having an index of zero. The Gini index of income concentration for families is de-

[2] United States Bureau of the Census, *United States Census of Population 1950*, Vol. II, Pt. 32, pp. XXVII-XXVIII; New York State Department of Commerce, *Personal Income in Counties of New York State 1964* (Albany: 1966), p. 2.

rived by subtracting from one the cumulative multiplicative sum of families and incomes. The formula is:

$$G = 1 - \Sigma_1 (f_{i+1} - f_i)(y_i + y_{i+1})$$

where y is income and f is families. An example of the computation when the distribution is equal follows:

$$G = 1.00 - \Sigma\ (.20{-}0)\ (.20{+}0)\ +\ (.40{+}.20)\ (.40\ {+}.20)\ +$$
$$(.60{-}.40)\ (.60{+}.40)\ \ +\ \ (.80{-}.60)\ \ (.80{+}.60)\ \ +$$
$$(1.00{-}.80)\ (1.00{+}.80)$$
$$G\ =\ 1.00{-}(.20)\ (.20{+}.60{+}1.00{+}1.40{+}1.80)$$
$$G\ =\ 1.00{-}(.20)\ (5.00)$$
$$G\ =\ 1.00{-}1.00\ =\ \underline{\underline{0.00}}$$

The Gini index of concentration, unlike the interdecile index, requires an estimate of the mid-point of each income class. Following the suggestion of the United States Bureau of the Census, the mid-point of the open-end class for the United States Census of Population income data was assumed to be $44,000 in 1959 and $20,000 in 1949.[3] The United States Census of Population data on incomes and population are used in the statistical analysis of income distribution in the Region.

Another measure which is used in the analysis is the concentration coefficient—the ratio of two percentages; *e.g.,* the per cent regional manufacturing employment is of regional total employment divided by the per cent national manufacturing employment is of national total employment. A ratio of 1.00 indicates a proportionate relationship between the region and the nation in that characteristic.

Regional Income Studies

A review of regional income studies is in order at this point. Hopefully, such a review will provide hints for further study as well as point to the independent variables which need to be considered if regional income differentials are to be explained. There are only a small number of such studies and there is little disagreement in the results which they obtained.

---

[3] United States Bureau of the Census, *Trends in the Income of Families and Persons in the United States: 1947 to 1960.* (Washington, D.C.: United States Government Printing Office, 1963), p. 24.

8

Demographic Variables

The influences of community size, labor force participation rates—persons fourteen years old or older in the labor force as a per cent of all persons in the age class—age, race, and sex on regional per capita income are significant but not conclusive—at least when taken separately. There is some tendency for per capita regional incomes to increase with city population size,[4] though the relative variations within the community-size classes are very large. Thompson provides some indication that this relationship may be diminishing.[5] The theoretical basis for the relationship is not clear.

Labor force participation rates are a second explanatory variable in regional income analysis. The relative variation of participation income per worker is some two-thirds less than participation income per person.[6] Hanna's use of over fifteen years of age population in computing "per capita" income provided the same results. The direction of the relationship is positive — relatively higher labor force participation rates are associated with relatively higher regional incomes.

The racial composition of the region's population is a third important demographic variable. The relative variation of per capita incomes is less for urban-white than rural-white persons.[7] A larger proportion of urban-white persons in a region is associated with a higher regional per capita income.

Hanna indicates that low male earnings and low female earnings are associated and thus are also associated with low per capita income.[8] Moreover, for low income regions the reported earnings

---

[4] Edwin Mansfield, "City Size and Income, 1949", *Regional Income* (New York: National Bureau of Economic Research, 1957), pp. 271-317; and Harvey S. Perloff, Edgar S. Dunn, Jr., Eric E. Lampard, and Richard F. Muth, *Regions, Resources, and Economic Growth* (Baltimore: The Johns Hopkins Press, 1960), chap. 27.

[5] Wilbur R. Thompson, *A Preface to Urban Economics* (Baltimore: The Johns Hopkins Press, 1965), p. 192, figure 76.

[6] Perloff, *et. al., Regions, Resources, and Economic Growth*, chap. 30.

[7] *Ibid.,* chap. 27.

[8] Frank A. Hanna, *State Income Differentials, 1919-1954* (Durham: Duke University Press, 1959), p. 133.

were less than what the females in the low income areas would have received if they had been paid the national average wage for their occupations.[9] Thus the sex of the labor force as well as its age and size relative to the total population may be important variables in explaining regional income differentials, but they are not the only variables.

Industrial and Occupational Structures

Hanna's study using rate constants provides conclusions which are important for this brief review. Using rate constant industry earnings multiplied by the employment weights for each industry in the separate states provides a summary measure for wage-salary income which can be compared to the reported wage-salary earnings per worker. One conclusion of the analysis indicates that regions with a concentration of high-paying industires tend to pay above industry average wages-salaries. Thus, one has the phenomenon of high-paying manufacturers being concentrated in a region, and the wage-salary rates for all manufacturing employees in the region being higher than industrial wage rates paid in the nation.[10] Explanation of this phenomenon is disaggregated into two parts: The industry concentrations are assumed to reflect comparative cost conditions while the wage-salary rates are assumed to be a result of factor proportions and are discussed in greater detail below.

This double advantage — a favorable industry structure and an above average wage-salary rate schedule — also is found when occupations are used in the rate constant analysis. This result also obtains when occupations of males are analyzed separately from those of females.[11] The importance of these phenomena are indicated by a coefficient of determination of $+.87$ between the reported earnings and the rate constant earnings by occupation. The occupational structure is another likely candidate for a variable to explain regional income differentials.

---

[9] *Ibid.*, p. 131 and appendix B.

[10] *Ibid.*, chap. 6.

[11] *Ibid.*, chap. 5.

10

Inter-Industry Analysis

Measured differentials in earnings within the same industry also require analysis. The likely candidate for an explanatory variable is capital per worker. That is, trade theory in economics does suggest that, *ceteris paribus,* the greater the amount of capital used relative to labor, the higher will be the marginal physical product of labor which, with a constant price of the product, will provide higher *rates* of earning for labor.[12] For agriculture, the relationship measured by a rank correlation coefficient is $+.88$ between capital per worker and output per worker; in addition, there is no systematic variation in agricultural income measured after capital per worker is included. Thus capital per worker in agriculture is another important variable in explaining regional income differentials.[13]

Manufacturing earnings rates also differ between regions, even after disaggregation to a two-digit S.I.C. level. Again, capital per worker is expected to be a significant explanatory variable. By using the assumption that the difference between total value added in an industry and total employee earnings is the earnings of capital, it is possible to identify the relative amounts of capital in each industry. The rank correlation coefficient was significant between per cent employed in capital intensive industries and earnings per employee.[14]

Since there is a scarcity of industry-capital data, it is not certain that capital is a significant explanatory variable in differential income analysis for each industry. But by extension, it is assumed to be of importance though the lack of data prevents any significant use of the assumption.

Other Income

The discussion above was, for the most part, focused on earnings or participation income, not the lesser components in per capita in-

---

[12] George H. Borts, "The Equalization of Returns and Regional Economic Growth", *American Economic Review,* June, 1960, pp. 319-47.

[13] Perloff, *et. al., Regions, Resources, and Economic Growth,* chap. 31.

[14] *Ibid.,* chap. 32.

come. Several brief statements can be made to remove this discrepancy. First, property income is highly correlated with participation income — +.84 rank correlation coefficient; secondly, participation income plus property income account for about ninety-five per cent of per capita personal income; third, the residual, transfer payments are unrelated to production income; *i.e.,* participation plus property income.[15]

Transfer payments tend to be an equalizing force on each individual's income: that is at least part of the reason for their existence. But the question raised here is whether such payments are regionally equalizing, and this depends on the relative rate of payment in each region and the relative number of persons who receive such payments. For example, a higher per capita income region may be expected to make a relatively large payment per person and have permissive regulations concerning the qualifications of persons who may receive old age assistance, unemployment compensation, and other transfer payments. In fact, the per capita social security payment in California for 1949 was four times that in Mississippi — the rates of per capita personal income in the two states were about two-and-a-half to one.[16] The opposite effect was measured for veterans' transfer payments.[17] The different result of the latter program is largely attributed to (1) the similarily in the characteristics of the program among the states with a relatively larger payment and (2) more persons receiving the payments in the lower income states. Thus transfer payments need be considered in the analysis of regional income differentials.

Migration

Out-migration could aid increases in a region's income — and lack of out-migration could aid decreases or stagnation of personal

---

[15] *Ibid.,* chap. 27.

[16] Howard G. Schaller, "Social Security Transfer Payments and Differences in State Per Capita Incomes, 1929, 1939, 1949", *Review of Economics and Statistics,* February, 1955, pp. 83-89.

[17] Howard G. Schaller, "Veterans Transfer Payments and State Per Capita Income, 1929, 1939, and 1949", *Review of Economics and Statistics,* November, 1953, pp. 325-32.

income in a region. By decreasing the availability of labor, a region's rate of earnings may be increased when less labor is combined with capital. The amount of out-migration necessary to raise a region's per capita income to a national average will depend on: (1) the rate of natural increase in the population, (2) the rate of in-migration, (3) the ratio of labor force to population, (4) the rate of underemployment and unemployment, (5) the "natural" rate of decline in demand for labor, and (6) the "natural" rate at which new jobs are being created. The region of concern is the labor market rather than the political region since jobs may be filled by commuters. Though large out-migration rates are associated with low income areas, the positive effect on regional income tends to be diminished by high birth rates.[18] The relative availability of labor continues to be higher in low income areas largely because of this phenomenon.

In summary, there are a host of variables which need be considered if regional income differentials are to be explained. Undoubtedly, some of the variables are interrelated — e.g., high birth rates and race — but each may have uniqueness for a policy or program. Of greater importance for this study is whether the variables which are discussed above also are significant when regional per capita income change is the dependent variable.

Regional Income Change

Per capita regional income changes depend upon the same variables as were discussed above, albeit the relationships tend to border on the statistically insignificant, given the faulty data now available.[19] Since this monograph is a study of only one six-county region, we cannot hope to provide tests of hypotheses which are relevant for a large number of regions, though the tests may be interesting in the formulation of more general hypotheses. The discussion of regional income growth hypotheses is separated into two parts: a discussion of changes in the size of regional per capita income and a discussion of

[18] Perloff, et. al., Regions, Resources, and Economic Growth, chap. 33.
[19] Ibid., p. 535.

changes in the composition of regional income. The separation is pedagogic rather than behavioral.

Changes In Total Income

Changes in the level of regional per capita income can be measured by a growth rate — an annual average rate of change — which is derived from the formula: $(1 + r)^N = (X_m/X_n)$ where r is the average annual percent change, N is the time period in years elapsed, and X_m/X_n is the per cent increase in the data. Alternatively, the growth rate can be derived from an 'Amount of 1 At Compound Interest' table. A prepared table was used for the growth rates reported herein.[20]

At first glance it appears that if the growth rate for total personal income in the Region was 2.1 per cent — as it was for 1948-1964 in constant prices — then the same growth rate might be expected for each type and source of income in the Region. That is, if participation and non-participation income in the Region each increased at a 2.1 per cent rate, then total personal income would have increased at a 2.1 per cent rate. Growth theories — such as base/service, Harrod-Domar, or others — suppose that such balance in the separate components is maintained.[21] The focus of growth theories is on the initiating force or exogenous variable which provides the change; *e.g.,* exports, investment, or productivity. But there are many exogenous or partly exogenous variables in an open economy. The very connotation of an open economy, which a region in the United States must be, is this: Each regional variable is only partly determined by other regional variables. For example, the regional rate of population growth is only partly determined by the regional birth rate and the regional death rate; regional employment is determined only partly by local sales; regional tax revenues are determined only partly by local tax rates. There are many more examples, but all to-

---

[20] R. S. Burington, *Handbook of Mathematical Tables and Formulas* (Sandusky, Ohio: Handbook Publishers, Inc., 1950), Table XIX.

[21] J. Thomas Romans, *Capital Exports and Growth Among U.S. Regions* (Middletown, Connecticut: Wesleyan University Press, 1965), chap. 5; and R. A. Siegel, "The Economic Base and Multiplier Analysis," *Urban Affairs Quarterly,* December, 1966, p. 37.

gether they imply that growth theories which assume that changes in composition do not occur are misleading.

It is probably of greater importance that the available growth theories require data which are not easily available. Capital/output ratios are not available from published data, nor are output/export ratios. Therefore, it is more reasonable, given the theory and the available data, to discuss changes in total regional income after changes in the composition of regional income, employment, and demography are analyzed.

Thus the above questions which asked first why the level of regional per capita income lagged behind that of the nation and second if the lagged regional income reflected decreasing efficiency is now re-phrased as follows: "Given that total personal regional income in-creased at a 2.1 per cent rate in the Mohawk Region during 1948-1964, and that regional population increased at a 1.1 per cent rate, such that per capita regional income increased at a 1.0 per cent rate, is this more than could have been expected when income and em-ployment in each regional industry changed at its respective national rate?" Since not all regional income is regionally employment related; *i.e.,* property income and other income are somewhat independent of the size and composition of regional industry, then the central ques-tion need be expanded to include the latter types of income. But the perspective is maintained that changes in the size of a regional economy can only be described and analyzed by first studying the changes in the region's composition *vis-a-vis* changes in the nation's composition.

Changes In Composition

Compositional changes can be analyzed through use of the shift technique which explicity includes national compositional changes as part of the computations. Thus differentials from national composi-tional changes can be computed, and important differentials — pos-sible sources of differentials in totals — can be observed and sub-jected to analysis. Chapters Two, Three and Four of this mono-graph use the shift technique extensively.

The shift technique is a standardization technique developed specifically for regional analysis. It employs three classes of data —

national total per cent change, national sector per cent change, and regional sector per cent change — and involves three computations — the regional sector original base multiplied sequentially by the national total per cent change, the national sectoral per cent change, and the regional sectoral per cent change. An example of the computations follows:

	1940-1960 Per cent Change	Absolute Data 1940	1960	Change
National Employment				
All Industry	29.980			
Industry I	56.073			
Regional Employment				
Industry I	93.959	2268	4399	2131
Standard Shifts X 2268				
All Industry	29.980		680	
National Industry I	56.073-29.980		592	
Regional Industry I	93.959-56.073		859	
Total				2131

That is, if Industry I in the region had increased at the All Industry average per cent change, Industry I would have gained 680 employees. If Industry I in the region had increased at the National Industry I per cent change, Industry I would have gained 592 employees, plus the 680 employees which were subtracted, or 1272 employees in total. In fact, Regional Industry I increased in employment by 2131 employees or 859 more employees than the standard gain. The Regional Industry I shift in employment was over one-third of the total increase and some two-thirds of the standard increase. Whether this above standard gain in regional employment is significant depends on the total size of the region's employment.[22]

---

[22] The best discussion of the shift technique is contained in Lowell D. Ashby, "Regional Change in a National Setting," Staff Working Paper in Economics and Statistics, No. 7, United States Department of Commerce, April, 1964. More limited discussions are available in: Walter Isard, *et. al., Methods of Regional Analysis* (Cambridge: The M. I. T. Press, 1960), p. 259; United States Department of Commerce, *Growth Patterns in Employment by County, 1940-1950 and 1950-1960,* Vol. II (Washington, D.C.: 1965), pp. xi-xviii; and C. J. Choguill and B. C. Cohen, "Unemployment Bias and Employment Shift Analysis," *Land Economics,* May, 1966, pp. 233-35.

While the shift technique can be applied to any type of data, it is of most importance in the following analysis when applied to wages and salaries, value added, and employment by industry source. The emphasis on these three types of data derives from their interdependence. Transforming the per cent changes into growth rates — a simple artithmetic transformation — permits the following statement: The growth rate in value added minus the growth rate in employment equals the growth rate in productivity or value added per employee. Moreover, the growth rate in value added will be equal to the growth rate in total wages and salaries and the growth rate in gross proprietors income if the shares of the latter in value added are constant.

With the use of these variables the ordinary content of microeconomic theory becomes useful. For example, if relative prices are constant, then a more rapid than national standard increase in Regional Industry I value added can be connected to either rapid increases in productivity or employment. If productivity increased more rapidly than employment, then, on the basis of micro-economic theory, rapid increases in rates of pay are expected. This theory provides that value added divided by employment equals the rate of pay for employees plus or minus the return to ownership or gross proprietor's income. If value added is increasing while employment is remaining relatively constant, then the rate of employee's pay is expected to increase.

When this analytical technique is used for each regional industry, the effects of national compositional changes on regional income-employment can be described. The process is laborious, but it does lead to statements concerning the composition of the regional economy, the effects of national compositional changes on the regional economy, and conclusions concerning the total response of the regional economy and the efficiency of its performance.

Hypotheses

Given the simple fact of a 1.0 per cent growth rate in regional per capita income vs. a 1.8 per cent growth rate in the nation, the following are relevant hypotheses:

1. Lagged income growth in the Mohawk Region did exist in the period 1940-1964, and a lower rate of per capita income growth in the Region was registered even after allowance for the Region's composition;

2. The lower rate of growth in per capita regional income was accompanied by standard increases in productivity;

3. Rates of growth in value added were seriously below those in the nation and this was translated into absolute decreases or relatively small increases in employment with below average increases in payroll per employee;

4. With the lack of increases in employment there were large amounts of out-migration, especially of the young and educated;

5. Out-commutation increased with the lack of increase in regional employment opportunities;

6. Demographic characteristics of the Region were altered with the lack of growth in employment opportunities such that the percentages of the population who are elderly, youthful, unemployed, and/or non-white increased;

7. Women entered the labor force in increasing numbers;

8. The types of income changed in composition such that non-wage income increased in percentage;

9. Gross proprietor's income increased at a lesser rate than in the nation;

10. Capital increased at a lesser rate than in the nation while the rate of return on capital also increased at a lower rate;

11. The distribution of income in the Region became more equal but at a lesser rate than in comparable regions.

The basic focus is the lack of income growth, given the composition of the regional economy and the changes in composition of the national economy.

The above are testable hypotheses. The final chapter of this monograph reviews the hypotheses and indicates the degree to which they must be recast. The following three chapters examine the data and describe the changes in the economic welfare of the Mohawk Region.

18

CHAPTER 2

The Study Region

The Mohawk Region — the area selected for analysis — is composed of six Upstate New York counties: Fulton, Hamilton, Herkimer, Lewis, Montgomery, and Oneida. As indicated by the map on page 20, the Region is located in the north central section of New York State, and has a total land area of 6,615 square miles. The geographic and economic diversity of this Region, including as it does a "forever wild" area established by the State Constitution and one of the State's seven Standard Metropolitan Statistical Areas (SMSA),[1] provides interesting comparisons for the type of regional economic study being undertaken here.

The sparsely-populated northern portion of the Mohawk Region lies in the Adirondack Mountains, while the southern portion of the Region encompasses the major part of the Mohawk River Valley and contains the Region's major population concentrations. This divergence of land form and elevation contributes to the Mohawk Region's variations in scenery, natural resources, and types of industrial activity.

The scenic resources of the northern Region serve as a base for a sizable tourist and recreation industry. An increasingly large number of persons find this area a desirable summer residence, and, this trend will continue as populations increase in adjacent areas and expanded highway facilities make larger portions of the area readily accessible. The same large forested areas which attract tourism

---

[1] Herkimer and Oneida counties form the Utica-Rome SMSA. Each SMSA is established by the United States Bureau of the Budget.

20

Map B - 1 Location of Mohawk Region and Constituent Counties

Counties:

F — Fulton
Ha — Hamilton
He — Herkimer
L — Lewis
M — Montgomery
O — Oneida

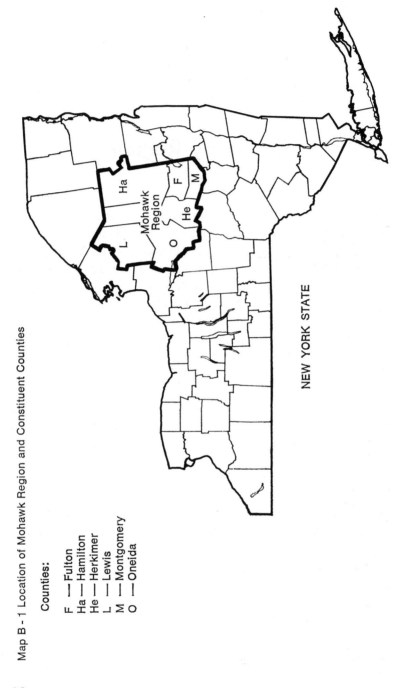

also support a forest-based industry. Lumbering and pulping, along with outdoor recreation, make up the major industrial activities of the upper Mohawk Region.

The inclusion of a major share of the upper Mohawk Region in the Adirondack State Park and Forest Preserve has precluded any intensive population settlement in this area. Hamilton County is among the largest counties of the State, but it is, at the same time, the least populous county.[2]

All six of the Mohawk Region's urban places of 10,000 or more population are situated in the southern section of the Region.[3] Dominating the Region's statistical picture is the Utica-Rome SMSA. In 1960, some seventy-one per cent of the Mohawk Region's population lived in this SMSA.

The lower part of the Region — which straddles the Mohawk River, the State Barge Canal, and the New York Thruway — has developed a much more diversified industrial base than has the upper part. Its location in regard to these sea level transportation routes across New York State has placed it in an advantageous position to attract industry. Manufacturing activity has been centered in the production of textiles, apparel, and leather goods, but in recent years there has been a growth in employment in machinery, electronics, and fabricated metals manufacturing.

Agriculture, particularly dairying, has a significant role throughout the Region. Four of the Region's six counties — Oneida, Herkimer, Montgomery, and Lewis — rank among the nation's one hundred leading dairy-producing counties, and along with meeting its own dairy needs, the Region is a major supplier for the New York metropolitan area. Other important agricultural specialties of the Mohawk Region include livestock associated with dairy farming, poultry, and vegetables.

---

[2] Of the 6,615 square miles of the Mohawk Region, 1,821 square miles are in the Adirondack State Park, and this includes almost all of the northern portion of the Region. Hamilton County is the only county in the State which is entirely within the Park's boundaries.

[3] These six urban places whose population numbered 10,000 or more in 1960 are Amsterdam, Gloversville, Johnstown, Ilion, Utica, and Rome.

Historical Development

Much of the early economic development of the Region is tied directly to the sea-level route for westward travel through the Appalachian Mountains offered by the Mohawk River and its Valley. After the settlement of Manhattan and the development of the Hudson Valley by the Dutch, the next available lands were in the Mohawk Valley and the territories beyond. Many persons, using the River and Valley as a western passage, found the level stretches of the Valley suitable for farming and remained there instead.

The Revolutionary War saw a movement of persons out of the Region, but with the cessation of hostility many of the old settlers returned to the Region. They were accompanied by an influx of colonists who previously had settled on the eastern seaboard and now were moving onto new lands made secure by the victory in the Revolution. Many of the new settlers were Palatine Germans who continued to follow their traditional vocations of cattle raising and dairy farming, while the migrating colonists brought their previous experiences in the industries and crafts of colonial existence to bear on the economy of the Mohawk Region.

Development of the Region's economy, from one based on self-sufficient domestic production to one based on commercial production for a market, was the result of a number of occurrences. Paramount in importance were: the completion and opening of the Erie Canal in 1825, widespread introduction of the power loom, and increased demand for forest products. The history and economic impact of the Erie Canal and the later railroad lines paralleling its route have received considerable attention in works dealing with American economic development, and little need be added in this brief summary. With the introduction of the power loom, textile production became centered in factories replacing the existent "cottage" production. Textiles, dairy farming, leather working, and forest products — the four industries which contributed most strongly in the development of the Mohawk Region — were all extensions or out-growths of earlier domestic production and were based on skills and techniques developed during the colonial period of relative self-sufficiency.

Existent water power provided by the Mohawk River stimulated the growth of the textile industry throughout the valley, while the fertile grazing lands and the traditional agricultural pursuits of the inhabitants provided the firm base for the dairying and cheesemaking industries which evolved in the Region. The extensive forests of the northern part of the Mohawk Region — the Lewis, Hamilton, and northern Herkimer Counties of today — were the foundation of the lumber and other forest products industries which developed. These same forests provided the furs and pelts which, along with the hides provided by the dairy farming, became the raw materials for the extensive leather and glove industry which developed in the Region, most particularly in Fulton County.

These industries, then, were the conerstones of industrial development for the Mohawk Region during the nineteenth century, and they developed patterns of organization and employment which continue to dominate the regional economy. The economic imbalances caused by this domination have only recently begun to be redressed.

The textile industry reached its highpoint in the Region during the first decade of the twentieth century, and then experienced a continuing decline during the 1920's which was partially a result of the noticeable movement of textile firms to the southeast. This decline was followed by the general economic collapse of the 1930's, and then the artificial stimulation in demand experienced during the wartime period of the 1940's. With the return to "normalcy" in the late 1940's and 1950's, the regional textile industry found itself once again in a weak competitive position facing rapidly changing consumer demands.

Just as adjustment in the textile industry was required by the introduction of a new range of synthetic materials, new technology, and shifts in consumer tastes, the leather industry in the Mohawk Region was required to meet the same set of forces. The Region still remains the leading center for the production of leather gloves in the United States, but it has had to adjust to rapid increases in competitive imports, changes in taste, changes in technology, and the widespread use of leather-like substitutes.

Dairy farming has maintained its place of dominance in the agriculture of the Region. Agriculture has tended to follow the national trends, but with a noticeable lag, so that the agricultural decline which has taken place in the Region tends to be less drastic in relation to national change. Specialization in dairy farming, with its trend toward

23

high capital investment, resulted in a continuing decline in agricultural employment.

The center of lumbering and lumber-based activities has undergone a series of geographic shifts in the United States since the fostering of these activities by the English in the early colonial period. Changing technology fostered by the depletion of forest reserves has caused the center of activity to shift from the northeastern and midwestern United States to the Far West and Southeast. The adoption of scientific forestry practices and the regrowth of depleted forest land has assured the continuation of a forest-based industry in the Mohawk Region, but to nowhere near the extent to which this industry existed in the early nineteenth century.[4]

Demographic and Economic Character

The focus of this study is the changes which have taken place in the regional economy during the 1940 to 1964 period. Variations in the availability of reliable statistical data have made it necessary to present time series of differing lengths. To provide a fuller picture of the place of the regional economy in the state and national economy, regional characteristics have been compared to those for the nation, New York State, and Upstate New York.[5]

Population of the Mohawk Region

The half million people of the Mohawk Region represented less than three per cent of the total state population in 1960, though the Region comprised sixteen per cent of the State's land area. During the twenty-year period, 1940-1960, the Region had been decreasing in its share of both New York State and Upstate population.

The changes which took place in the relative position of the regional population are a reflection of the differential rates of population

---

[4] Nelson Greene, *History of Mohawk Valley, 1614-1925* (Chicago: S. J. Clarke Co., 1925); V. C. Crisafulli, "Economic Development Efforts in the Utica-Rome, New York Area," *Community Economic Development Efforts* (New York: Committee for Economic Development, 1964).

[5] The Upstate designation is given for New York State exclusive of the nine counties comprising the New York SMSA. Much of the data in the succeeding chapters were taken from Richard J. Kalish and Donald J. Reeb, *An Economic Study of the Adirondack-Mohawk Region* (Albany: New York State Office of Planning Coordination, 1966).

Table B-1

Population and Population Distribution *
1960 and 1940

	Population Size 1960	Population Size 1940	Per cent Share 1960	Per cent Share 1940	Per cent Share 1960	Per cent Share 1940
Nation (000)	178,464	131,669	——	——	——	——
New York (000)	16,782	13,479	100.0	100.0	——	——
Upstate (000)	6,088	4,772	36.3	35.4	100.0	100.0
Region	466,831	397,905	2.8	3.0	7.7	8.3
SMSA	330,771	263,163	2.0	2.0	5.4	5.5

* United States Bureau of the Census, *United States Census of Population 1960*, Vol. I, Pt. 34, Table 6; Pt. 1, Table 1; *United States Census of Population 1950*, Vol. II, Pt. 32, Table 5.

growth[6] which took place during 1940-1960 for the various areas. For each of the time periods computed, the Region displayed a rate of

Table B-2

Rate of Population Growth *
1960-1940

	1960-1940 (Per Cent)	1960-1950 (Per Cent)	1950-1940 (Per Cent)
Nation	1.5	1.7	1.4
New York	1.1	1.3	1.0
Upstate	1.2	1.4	1.0
Region	.8	1.0	.5
SMSA	1.1	1.5	.8

* United States Bureau of the Census, *United States Census of Population 1960*, Vol. I, Pt. 34, Table 6; Pt. 1, Table 1; *United States Census of Population 1950*, Vol. II, Pt. 32, Table 5.

population growth conspicuously below that of the nation and the State. Had the Mohawk Region grown at a rate similar to that established by the nation, one could have expected a regional population of

---

[6] The growth rates used here always will refer to per cent changes computed by the following formula: $(1 + r)^n = Xm/Xn$ where r is the annual average per cent change, N is the time period elapsed and Xm/Xn is the per cent increase reflected by the data.

25

539,884 persons in 1960. In actuality, the population was 466,831, or 48.6 per cent of the expected gain. On the basis of national population growth, the Region lost 73,053 persons to the nation during the 1960-1940 period.

Table B-3

Shift in Population*
1960-1940

	Expected Gain in Population 1960 (Based on National Rate)	Actual Gain in Population 1960-1940	Difference (Actual —Expected)	Realized Per Cent of Expected
Nation	46,794,961	46,794,961	——	——
New York	4,809,591	3,303,162	—1,506,429	68.7
Upstate	1,702,812	1,315,446	—387,366	77.3
Region	141,979	68,926	—73,053	48.6
SMSA	93,528	67,608	—25,920	72.3

* Based on Tables B-1 and B-2.

Since the land area of the Region has remained constant subsequent to 1940, the rate of growth of population density was identical with the rate of growth of population: the growth in density was .8 per cent per year.

Knowledge that the Mohawk Region gained 68,926 persons during the twenty-year period under investigation provides only an idea of the magnitude and direction of change which occurred. If one is attempting to understand the nature and composition of the changes which took place in the regional population structure rather than simply the changes in the level of population, it is necessary to dis-aggregate and examine the population changes by demographic characteristics.

The population of the Mohawk Region is disaggregated in the following pages and tables and compared with the three comparison areas on the basis of eight characteristics: age; sex; race and nativity; urban, rural non-farm, and rural farm place of residence; vital statistics; marital status; household composition; and education. To standardize comparisons, concentration coefficients have been constructed.[7]

Sex and Age Characteristics

As of 1960, the age distribution of the study Region's population was markedly different from that displayed for the nation. The Mohawk Region had a significantly higher proportion of persons sixty-five years of age and over — 30.4 per cent — and a notable deficiency of persons in age categories below sixty-five. New York State and the Upstate area exhibited a general pattern similar to that of the Region, but with some noticeable variation.

Table B-4

Age Distribution of Population *
1960

	1960 Per cent Distribution			1960 Concentration Coefficient		
	0-17 Years	18-64 Years	65 years and over	0-17 Years	18-64 Years	65 years and over
Nation	35.8	55.0	9.2	1.000	1.000	1.000
New York	34.6	54.6	10.8	.966	.993	1.174
Upstate	31.8	58.1	10.1	.888	1.056	1.098
Region	34.3	53.7	12.0	.958	.976	1.304
SMSA	34.6	54.2	11.3	.966	.986	1.228

* United States Bureau of the Census, *United States Census of Population 1960,* Vol. I, Pt. 34, Tables 13, 48 and 82; Pt. 1, Table 155.

---

[7] A concentration coefficient is analogous to the location quotient developed by Daniel Creamer while with the United States National Resources Planning Board and used extensively by P. Sargant Florence and others.
Its form is $Si/Sn \div Ni/Nn$ where:

Si = Number of persons displaying characteristic in Region
Sn = Number of persons in Region
Ni = Number of persons displaying characteristic in United States
Nn = Number of persons in United States

Thus, the concentration coefficient is a ratio of two ratios. When the coefficient is greater than one (1.000) it indicates that the characteristic among the population in the region is relatively more plentiful than in the nation, while a coefficient less than one indicates the opposite. For further details, see Walter Isard, *et. al., Methods of Regional Analysis.* (Cambridge: The M. I T. Press, 1960), p. 124.

Table B-5

Median Age of Population *
1960, 1950, 1940

	1960	1950	1940
Nation	29.5	30.2	29.0
New York	33.1	33.7	32.2
Upstate	31.3	34.5	36.8
Region	31.7	34.8	35.4

* United States Bureau of the Census, *United States Census of Population 1960*, Vol. I, Pt. 34, Tables 16 and 27; Pt. 1, Table 47; *United States Census of Population 1950*, Vol. II, Pt. 32, Tables 15 and 41; *United States Census of Population 1940*, Vol. II, Pt. 3, Table 22; Vol. IV, Pt. 3, Table 3.

For the period under study, the median age of the population of the Mohawk Region experienced a considerable decrease, while that of the nation remained about constant. The reason for this regional decline can be traced to changes in age distribution; most particularly, the 0-17 year old age group increased in percentage of population in the Region.

A restatement of the structural change in the age composition of the Mohawk Region in absolute terms presents a more vivid picture than that indicated by the use of percentage figures.

Table B-6

Absolute Change in Regional Age Composition *
1960-1940

Age Groups	Absolute Change 1960-1940	Total Change 1960-1940
0-17	+ 55,873	
18-64	− 5,165	
65 and over	+ 18,218	68,926

* United States Bureau of the Census, *United States Census of Population 1960*, Vol. I, Pt. 34, Tables 16 and 27; Pt. 1, Table 47; *United States Census of Population 1950*, Vol. II, Pt. 32, Tables 15 and 41; *United States Census of Population 1940*, Vol. II, Pt. 3, Table 22; Vol. IV, Pt. 3, Table 3.

The ratio of males to females in the study region shows a direction of change similar to that of the State and nation. The number of males per one hundred females had been decreasing throughout the twenty-year period. The rate at which this change took place does not show great variation among the four areas presented.

Table B-7

Males Per 100 Females*
1960, 1950, 1940

	1960 (Per Cent)	1950 (Per Cent)	1940 (Per Cent)
Nation	97.0	98.6	100.7
New York	93.8	95.4	98.6
Upstate	96.4	97.9	100.8
Region	96.3	97.8	100.7

* United States Bureau of the Census, *United States Census of Population 1960*, Vol. I, Pt. 34, Tables 16 and 27; Pt. 1, Table 47; *United States Census of Population 1950*, Vol. II, Pt. 32, Tables 15 and 41; *United States Census of Population 1940*, Vol. II, Pt. 3, Table 22; Vol. IV, Pt. 3, Table 3.

The disaggregation of population figures for 1960 according to sex and age distribution indicated that the middle population age group — 18-64 — of the Mohawk Region was more deficient in males than females when compared to national figures. Based on national percentages, the Region had 2.0 per cent too few males in this category, and 1.5 per cent too few females. It is important to note that this deficiency is in the age group usually viewed as the productive age group; *i.e.*, those forming the bulk of the available labor force.

Table B-8

Age and Sex Distribution of Regional Population*
1960

	Concentration Coefficient					
	0-17 Years		18-64 Years		65 Years and Over	
	Male	Female	Male	Female	Male	Female
Nation	1.000	1.000	1.000	1.000	1.000	1.000
Region	.958	.947	.980	.985	1.274	1.300

* United States Bureau of the Census, *United States Census of Population 1960*, Vol. I, Pt. 34, Tables 16 and 27; Pt. 1, Table 47; *United States Census of Population 1950*, Vol. II, Pt. 32, Tables 15 and 41; *United States Census of Population 1940*, Vol. II, Pt. 3, Table 22; Vol. IV, Pt. 3, Table 3.

The absolute change in the sex distribution of the Region's population for the 1940-1960 period is presented in Table B-9. These absolute figures indicate that the Region gained ten thousand more females than males.

Table B-9

Absolute Change in Number of Males and Females for Mohawk Region *
1960-1940

	Increase 1960-1940	Total Increase 1960-1940
Males	+29,475	
Females	+39,451	
		+68,926

* United States Bureau of the Census, *United States Census of Population 1960*, Vol. I, Pt. 34, Tables 16 and 27; Pt. 1, Table 47; *United States Census of Population 1940*, Vol. II, Pt. 3, Table 22; Vol. IV, Pt. 3, Table 3.

Nativity and Race

The nativity-race composition of the Region's population displays a marked difference from that of the State and nation. Persons of foreign stock[8] — all first and second generation Americans — make up a considerably larger per cent share of the Region's population — 28.4 per cent — than that of the nation — 19.3 per cent. Per cent share of foreign-born is also higher for the Region than for the United States. The non-white population constitutes a significantly smaller share of the whole population in the Mohawk Region than in either the nation or the State. Only 1.3 per cent of the Region's population in 1960 were classified as non-white.

The foreign-born portion of the Mohawk Region's population was a declining share of the total between 1940 and 1960, a trend experienced nationally as well as statewide. Changes which have been taking place in the Region's per cent share of foreign-born population have caused the Mohawk area to assume a nativity composition more closely resembling that of the nation.

---

[8] The designation "Foreign Stock" is of recent origin in the United States Census data, so time comparisons are not feasible.

Table B-10

Nativity and Race *
1960

	1960 Per Cent Foreign-Born	1960 Per Cent Foreign Stock	1960 Per Cent Non-white
Nation	5.4	19.3	11.2
New York	13.6	38.7	8.9
Upstate	7.1	26.8	3.4
Region	7.5	28.4	1.3
SMSA	7.6	29.2	1.6

* United States Bureau of the Census, *United States Census of Population 1960*, Vol. I, Pt. 34, Tables 13, 40, 72, 78, 79, and 89; and Vol. I, Pt. 1, Tables 66, 69, and 70.

Table B-11

Foreign-Born as a Per Cent of Total Population*
1960, 1950, 1940

	1960	1950	1940
Nation	5.4	6.9	8.8
New York	13.6	23.6	25.7
Upstate	7.1	9.2	10.4
Region	7.5	11.2	13.5
SMSA	7.6	11.6	13.7

* United States Bureau of the Census, *United States Census of Population 1960*, Vol. I, Pt. 34, Tables 13, 40, 72, 78, 79, and 89; and Vol. I, Pt. 1, Tables 66, 69, and 70.

Comparing changes in per cent foreign-born population between the Mohawk Region and the nation, the Region experienced a greater decline in per cent foreign-born than did the nation as a whole, and so the number of foreign-born persons in the Region in 1960 was less than could be expected had the Region followed the national pattern.

The Mohawk Region had a consistently lower proportion of non-white population throughout the twenty-year period examined than that displayed by either the nation or the State. As indicated by Table B-13, the growth rate of non-white population for the Region was

31

Table B-12

Expected and Actual Foreign-Born Population*
1960

	Actual Total	Expected Total (Based on Nation)	Difference
Region	35,012	44,762	−11,750

* United States Bureau of the Census, *United States Census of Population 1960*, Vol. I, Pt. 34, Tables 13, 40, 72, 78, 79, and 89; and Vol. I, Pt. 1, Tables 66, 69, and 70.

considerably higher than that for the nation and State, but it still constitutes a small per cent of the total population. The high regional growth rate is attributable to the small number of non-whites in the base year of 1940.

Table B-13

Per Cent Non-white Population and Growth Rate*
1960-1940

	Per Cent Non-White Population			Growth Rate
	1960	1950	1940	1940-1960 (Per Cent)
Nation	11.2	10.5	10.2	2.0
New York	8.9	6.5	4.4	3.6
Upstate	3.4	2.2	1.3	4.9
Region	1.3	.8	.4	6.1
SMSA	1.6	.9	.4	8.4

* United States Bureau of the Census, *United States Census of Population 1960*, Vol. I, Pt. 34, Tables 13, 48, and 82; Pt. 1, Table 66; *United States Census of Population 1950*, Vol. II, Pt. 32, Tables 10, 12, 15, and 41; *United States Census of Population 1940*, Vol. II, Pt. 3, Tables 4 and 22.

Had the Region's non-white population grown at the same rate as that of the nation, there would have been an increase of 2,423 non-whites in the regional population rather than the 6,069 increase which did take place.

Of the Region's 6,069 non-white population in 1960, 5,292 resided in the two counties constituting the Utica-Rome SMSA. The SMSA

Table B-14

Actual and Expected Non-white Population*
1960

	Actual Total	Expected Total (National Basis)	Difference
Region	6,069	2,423	+3,646

* United States Bureau of the Census, *United States Census of Population 1960*, Vol. I, Pt. 34, Tables 13, 48, and 82; Pt. 1, Table 66; *United States Census of Population 1950*, Vol. II, Pt. 32, Tables 10, 12, 15, and 41; *United States Census of Population 1940*, Vol. II, Pt. 3, Tables 4 and 22.

not only contained the bulk of the Region's non-white population in 1960, but, as indicated by the growth rates in Table B-13, gained non-white population at a greater than regional rate.

Urban, Rural Non-Farm, Rural Farm Population

The population settlement pattern of the Region in 1960 shows a dispersion similar to that of the upstate area, but at some variance to that of the nation. A smaller per cent share of the Mohawk population resides in areas classified as urban — sixty-five per cent as opposed to seventy per cent — while the rural non-farm residents made up a significantly larger share. Rural non-farm classification is composed of persons not classified as farmers residing in places of less than 2,500 inhabitants. Persons falling in this category constitute twenty-nine per cent of the regional population, compared to twenty-three per cent on the national level. This indicates a relatively greater dispersion of population in small clusters or on individual sites in the Region.

Changes which took place in settlement patterns are indicated in Table B-16. Comparisons are drawn for the 1950-1960 period because of substantial changes made in definitions and categories between 1940 and 1950.

Comparison of growth rates indicates that urbanization had been occurring at a considerably slower rate for the Region — 1.0 per cent — than for the United States — 2.6 per cent — and that the Region had reduced rural non-farm population comparable to the national decline.

33

Table B-15

Population Settlement Pattern*
1960

| | Per Cent Urban | Per Cent Rural Non-farm | Per Cent Rural Farm | Concentration Coefficient | | |
				Urban	Rural Non-farm	Rural Farm
Nation	69.9	22.6	7.5	1.000	1.000	1.000
New York	85.4	12.7	1.9	1.222	.562	.253
Upstate	64.2	30.6	5.2	.918	1.354	.693
Region	64.8	29.2	6.0	.927	1.292	.800
SMSA	70.2	22.6	4.6	1.004	1.115	.613

* United States Bureau of the Census, *United States Census of Population 1960*, Vol. I, Pt. 34, Tables 6, 71, and 91; Pt. 1, Table 3.

Table B-16

Growth Rates of Settlement*
1960-1950

	Urban (Per Cent)	Rural Non-Farm (Per Cent)	Rural Farm (Per-Cent)
Nation	2.6	1.7	−4.2
New York	1.3	3.1	−6.1
Upstate	1.4	3.7	−6.0
Region	1.0	2.6	−4.3
SMSA	1.7	3.1	−5.3

* United States Bureau of the Census, *United States Census of Population 1960*, Vol. I, Pt. 34, Tables 6, 71, and 91; Pt. 1, Table 3.

Vital Statistics

Birth and death rates for the Region did not differ significantly from those of the State or nation during the twenty-year period under investigation. The relative changes which took place are reflected in the changes which occurred in the age composition of the Mohawk Region's population.

Table B-17

Birth and Death Rates *
1960-1940

	Birth Rate (Per Cent)			Death Rate (Per Cent)		
	1960	1950	1940	1960	1950	1940
Nation	2.4	2.4	1.8	1.0	1.0	1.1
New York	2.1	2.0	1.5	1.1	1.1	1.1
Upstate	2.2	2.2	1.5	1.0	1.1	1.2
Region	2.2	2.1	1.6	1.1	1.1	1.3
SMSA	2.3	2.2	1.5	1.0	1.1	1.2

* New York State Department of Health, *Monthly Vital Statistics Review* (March, 1941), Table 23; *Seventy-First Annual Report,* December, 1950, Table 27; *Eighty-First Statistical Report,* December, 1960, Table 27.

A measure of rate of natural population increase can be derived with the use of birth and death rate data.[9] Subtraction of the death rate from the birth rate results in the rate of population increase, ignoring net migration. The results of this computation indicates a relatively lower rate of natural increase in the Mohawk Region than in the nation, another reflection of the lower rates of the Region's population growth.

Another measure commonly used to signify potential population growth is the fertility ratio. This is the ratio of the number of children 0-5 years of age per one hundred women 15-44 years of age in an area. Based on this measure, the potential natural population growth in the Mohawk Region was only slightly lower than that expected for the nation. A more reliable estimate of regional population increase must wait for the discussions of the effects of net population migration on the Region.

Marital Status and Household Composition

The marital status of persons fourteen years of age and over in the Mohawk Region generally resembles the pattern exhibited in the

---

[9] The formula is $Rb/Rp - Rd/Rp = Pn/Rp$ where:

Rb is the number of live births in a given year;
Rd is the number of deaths in the same year;
Rp is the population of the beginning of that year;
and Pn/Rp is the natural rate of population increase.

Table B-18

Rates of Natural Increase and Fertility Ratio*
1960

	Birth Rate (Per cent)	Death Rate (Per cent)	Rate of Natural Increase (Per cent)	Fertility Ratio
Nation	2.4	1.0	1.4	49
New York	2.2	1.1	1.1	42
Upstate	2.1	1.0	1.1	49
Region	2.2	1.1	1.1	48
SMSA	2.3	1.0	1.3	49

* New York State Department of Health, *Eighty-First Statistical Report,* December, 1960, Table 27; United States Bureau of the Census, *United States Census of Population 1960,* Vol. I, Pt. 1, Table 55; Pt. 34, Table 13.

United States, as does the per cent of the population residing in households.[10] Unrelated individuals and persons in group quarters account for 9.3 per cent of the Region's population (100.0-90.7) approximately two per cent fewer than the national figure.

Table B-19

Marital Status and Household Composition*
1960

	Per cent Married of Persons 14 Years Old and Over		Per cent of Population in		Average Household Size	Average Family Size
	Male	Female	Households	Families		
Nation	68.5	64.7	97.3	92.9	3.2	3.6
New York	69.2	64.9	97.2	89.9	3.3	3.7
Upstate	68.5	63.2	96.4	92.1	3.1	3.5
Region	69.1	65.9	96.4	90.7	3.3	3.7
SMSA	67.6	64.4	95.3	89.8	3.3	3.6

* United States Bureau of the Census, *United States Census of Population 1960,* Vol. I, Pt. 34, Tables 13, 48, and 82; Vol. I, Pt. 1, Tables 48, 49, and 50.

---

[10] The total population of an area is divided in the following manner regarding familial characteristics: total population = persons in group quarters+ persons in families + unrelated individuals not in group quarters; household population = persons in families + unrelated individuals in households.

The per cent shares of the regional population classified as unrelated individuals and persons in families remained relatively constant between 1950 and 1960. For the nation during this period, there was a two per cent decline in the proportion of unrelated individuals in the total population, and a slight increase in the per cent share of persons in families — 0.4 per cent. The remainder of the population is included in the statistics for persons in group quarters and institutional population. Due to some overlap in classification, institutional population cannot be considered as merely the residual of unrelated individuals and population in families taken from total population.

Education

The educational attainment of persons twenty-five years old and over in the Mohawk Region presents a pattern at some variance with that of the State and the nation. The Region had a relatively higher percentage of persons who completed grade school, but a smaller percentage who completed high school. This regional pattern is logically consistent and related to the age and nativity distribution existent in the Mohawk Region.

The percentage of persons completing no school at all, however, does not follow a consistent trend. The Mohawk Region was the only area of those listed in Table B-21 to experience an increase, between 1950 and 1960, in the per cent share of persons twenty-five years of age and over who completed no schooling. The explanation for this occurrence is not clear. It may be the result of the Region's age composition as opposed to that of the other areas, or perhaps, a result of the composition of migrating populations into and out of the Region. There appears to be little reliable data dealing with the educational attainment of migrating population for counties or regions.

A comparison of aggregate school enrollment for 1960 indicates that the Mohawk Region's total school enrollment as a percentage of total population was less than that for the nation. A portion of this difference in total percentages is due to the relatively small per cent of college enrollment for the Region. Adjustment for college enrollment

37

Table B-20

Educational Attainment of Persons 25 and Over[*]
1960

	Percent Completing Grade School	Percent Completing High School	Percent No School Completed
Nation	17.5	41.0	2.3
New York	18.8	40.9	3.5
Upstate	18.8	40.3	2.0
Region	20.8	36.8	3.4
SMSA	19.7	38.0	3.9

[*] United States Bureau of the Census, *United States Census of Population 1960*, Vol. I, Pt. 34, Tables 73 and 81; Pt. 1, Table 76.

Table B-21

Per Cent of Persons 25 Years and Over
with No School Completed[*]
1960, 1950, 1940

	1960 (Per cent)	1950 (Per cent)	1940 (Per cent)
Nation	2.3	2.6	3.7
New York	3.5	3.5	5.6
Upstate	2.0	2.0	3.0
Region	3.4	2.5	5.0
SMSA	3.9	4.1	4.1

[*] United States Bureau of the Census, *United States Census of Population 1960*, Vol. I, Pt. 34, Tables 73 and 81; Pt. 1, Table 76; *United States Census of Population 1950*, Vol. II, Pt. 32, Tables 34, 38, and 42; *United States Census of Population 1940*, Vol. II, Pt. 3, Tables 21, 30, 31, and F48.

lessens the difference between the Region and nation, but a difference continues to exist.[11]

---

[11] A portion of the lower per cent share of college enrollments for the Mohawk Region can be attributed to the method used in tabulating college enrollments in the 1960 Census of Population. During the period covered by this study, there were two small private colleges and one two-year public college in the Mohawk Region.

Table B-22

School Enrollment as a Per Cent of Total Population*
1960

| | Concentration Coefficient | | |
	Total Enrollment 5-34 Years of Age	Enrollment in Kindergarten Through High School	Enrollment in College
Nation	1.000	1.000	1.000
Region	.959	.987	.500

* United States Bureau of the Census, *United States Census of Population 1960*, Vol. I, Pt. 34, Tables 73 and 83; Pt. 1, Table 75.

In order to gain a clearer picture of the factors contributing to the Region's lower per cent share of school enrollments, concentration coefficients of school enrollments by age have been prepared. To construct these ratios, comparisons of age groups enrolled are taken as a percentage of total number of persons in the age group.

Table B-23

School Enrollment by Age*
1960

| | Concentration Coefficient | | | | | |
	5-6	7-13	14-15	16-17	18-19	20-34
Nation	1.000	1.000	1.000	1.000	1.000	1.000
Region	1.339	1.000	.997	1.009	1.288	.758

* United States Bureau of the Census, *United States Census of Population 1960*, Vol. I, Pt. 1, Table 73; Pt. 34, Table 83.

Excluding the twenty to thirty-four year-old age group, the bulk of the college population, the Region presents a better school enrollment pattern than when compared to the nation on a total basis. The only age group in which the Region does not meet the national average is the fourteen to fifteen year-old age group, and the difference is slight. Another factor brought out in Table B-23 is that the Region had a greater than national share of its sixteen to nineteen year-olds enrolled in school, which indicates that the Mohawk Region had a lower "drop-out" rate than the nation.

Extending our comparison of school enrollments by age to include New York State and the upstate area causes enrollments in the Mohawk Region to look less favorable. The Region had a smaller percentage of each of its age groups from fourteen to nineteen enrolled in school than did either New York State or upstate. Data examined do not allow one to infer whether the smaller enrollments in the eighteen to nineteen year-old category are due to a greater incidence of drop-outs or smaller percentages of students going on to college.

Table B-24

Percent Enrolled in School by Age Group*
1960

	Ages 14-15 (Per cent)	Ages 16-17 (Per cent)	Ages 18-19 (Per cent)
Nation	94.1	80.9	28.8
New York	94.9	82.1	43.1
Upstate	94.6	83.6	48.6
Region	93.8	81.6	37.1

* United States Bureau of the Census, *United States Census of Population 1960*, Vol. I, Pt. 1, Table 73; Pt. 34, Table 83.

Labor Force and Labor Force Participation

Residents of the Mohawk Region who reported themselves as in the labor force to the United States Bureau of the Census in 1960 numbered 186,972 or forty per cent of the population. The Mohawk Region, along with New York State, had a higher per cent share of its population in the labor force than did the nation. The Region has a higher crude participation rate — labor force as a per cent of total population — than either the United States or the upstate area. Adjustment of labor force participation rates to reflect "productive age" population[12] does not change the rank-order relationship displayed by the crude rates. Using either criteria, the Study Region had a total labor force participation rate greater than the nation.

---

[12] Some authors have held that a more meaningful picture of labor force participation can be gained by taking labor force as a per cent of productive population. Productive population is viewed as persons fourteen years old and over, the major income earning group.

Labor Force Characteristics. Analysis of labor force participation may be carried further by asking the question: "Were participation rates for the Region—based on population fourteen years and over—higher than national rates for both males and females?" The answer to this question, as provided by Table B-26, is both affirmative and negative. The Mohawk Region had a female participation rate which was higher than either the nation or state areas, and a male participation rate

Table B-25

Labor Force Participation *
1960

	Per cent of Total Population in Labor Force	Concentration Coefficient LF/TP	Per cent of Population 14 years & Over in Labor Force	Concentration Coefficient LF/Pop. 14+
Nation	39.0	1.000	55.3	1.000
New York	41.7	1.076	56.5	1.022
Upstate	39.3	1.009	55.0	.995
Region	40.0	1.028	55.9	1.011
SMSA	39.1	1.003	54.9	.993

* United States Bureau of the Census, *United States Census of Population 1960*, Vol. I, Pt. 34, Tables 20, 27, 33, 36, 73, and 83; Pt. 1, Table 84.

which was lower than any of these areas. It was the high rate of labor force participation by females which caused the Region to have a higher than national rate of total labor force participation.

Table B-26

Labor Force Participation by Sex *
1960

	Participation Rates Male	Female	Concentration Coefficient Male	Female
	(Per cent)			
Nation	77.4	34.5	1.000	1.000
New York	78.1	37.0	1.000	1.072
Upstate	76.4	35.2	.987	1.020
Region	75.8	37.4	.979	1.081
SMSA	75.2	35.9	.972	1.041

* United States Bureau of the Census, *United States Census of Population 1960*, Vol. I, Pt. 34, Tables 20, 27, 33, 36, 73, and 83; Pt. 1, Table 84.

Labor Force by Sex and Age. Based on national standards, male labor force participation in the Region took place at a higher rate only in the eighteen to twenty-four year-old age category. For each of the other age categories, the participation rate for males was lower regionally than nationally. Regional female participation, however, was higher than national for each age group except for fourteen to seven-

Table B-27

Labor Force Participation by Age and Sex *
1960

	Male Labor Force Participation by Age Group (Per cent)				Female Labor Force Participation by Age Group (Per cent)			
	14-17	18-24	25-64	65+	14-17	18-24	25-64	65+
Nation	26.6	80.0	92.5	30.5	14.0	45.3	42.5	10.3
Region	24.8	82.5	92.2	28.9	12.4	48.6	42.8	11.8
Concentration Coefficient	.932	1.031	.997	.948	.888	1.072	1.006	1.139

* United States Bureau of the Census, *United States Census of Population 1960*, Vol. I, Pt. 34, Tables 20, 27, 33, 36, 73, and 83; Pt. 1, Table 84.

teen year olds. It is possible to establish the absolute deviation of total regional participation from the national standard by establishing net differentials by age and sex.[13]

Having established the existence of a lower than national participation rate for males in the Mohawk Region, it is interesting to note that the absolute deviation in male participation is actually quite small. Net male participation was only 568 persons less than could be expected at national rates. Five hundred sixty-eight males constituted .47 per cent of the Region's male labor force (568÷122,127). The reasons for this deviation may be attributable to a host of factors, including the type of sampling used, pattern of school attendance, and composition of institutional population.

The absolute deviation for female participation, on the other hand,

---

[13] National participation rates for males and females by age category are applied to the regional totals, establishing an estimated participation for each category based on a national standard. The estimated participation then is compared to the actual participation in each category to establish regional deviations.

Table B-28

Absolute Deviations of Regional Labor Force Participation From National Standard*
1960

Age Group	Male	Female
14-17	−256	−213
18-24	+398	+564
25-64	−315	+3,755
65+	−395	+422
Total	−568	+4,548
Total Net Deviation	+3,980	

* United States Bureau of the Census, *United States Census of Population 1960*, Vol. I, Pt. 34, Tables 20, 27, 33, 36, 73, and 83; Pt. 1, Table 84.

is sizable, 4,548 more females than anticipated on the basis of nation-wide participation. This excess of 4,598 women participants is equivalent to 7.01 per cent of the Region's female labor force and is of large enough signifiance to warrant further examination.

Female Labor Force Participation 1960. Two factors believed to be indicative of the major reasons for the higher regional female participation rates are (1) the per cent of married women, with husbands present, in the labor force and (2) the per cent of the female population fourteen years and over who are enrolled in school and not in the labor force. A comparison of the national and regional percentages in each category is presented in Tables B-29 and B-30.

Table B-29

Married Women, With Husbands Present, in Labor Force*
1960

	Per cent	Concentration Coefficient
Nation	55.2	1.000
Region	59.5	1.078

* United States Bureau of the Census, *United States Census of Population 1960*, Vol. I, Pt. 1, Table 196; Part 34, Tables 116 and 183.

Application of the United States participation rate for married women in 1960 to the appropriate category of the married female population in the Mohawk Region provides the absolute difference in participation.

Actual Number of Married Females, Husband Present,
in Labor Force of Mohawk Region 38,593
Expected Number in Category at National Rate 35,794

Absolute Difference 2,799

The Region had 2,799 more married women, with husbands present, in the labor force than could have been expected given the national rate.

Table B-30

School Enrollment of Females 14 and Over Not in Labor Force*
1960

	Per cent of Age Group Enrolled in School	Concentration Coefficient
Nation	81.6	1.000
Region	69.4	.850

* United States Bureau of the Census, *United States Census of Population 1960*, Vol. I, Pt. 1, Tables 52 and 83.

The Region had a smaller per cent share of its female population fourteen years old and over enrolled in school and hence, most probably, more women in the labor force. Comparison of regional enrollments with expected enrollments at national standard provides the figure for absolute deviation.

Actual Enrollment of Females Fourteen and over in
School, Mohawk Region 12,006
Expected Enrollment at National Rate 14,127

Difference − 2,121

There were 2,121 fewer females fourteen years of age and older enrolled in schools in the Mohawk Region than could have been expected given United States standards.

44

It is not correct to assume that all females not enrolled in school are to be counted as in the labor force, nor can one assume that the two groups examined in these tables entirely account for the higher female participation rate of the Mohawk Region. Simple combination of the absolute differences established above gives a total figure of 4,920 females, which is 372 more than the number of extra women in the labor force — 4,548. A portion of the excess displayed in the total figure is due to an overlapping of the two groups, or double-counting. A portion of the women who were not enrolled in school were also married with their husbands present, and so are being counted twice through inclusion in both categories.

Had the standard used in these tables been the State or upstate area instead of the nation, the same general pattern of labor force participation would have been established. The effects of excess female participation on wage and salary income per capita in the Region will be examined in some length in the discussion of regional personal income.

Changes in the Labor Force 1960-1940. The regional labor force grew at a significantly lower rate than for any of the comparison areas, while the Region's rate of participation exceeded that of the nation for the entire period. Labor force participation rates were continually above the United States standard, but the relative difference between the two was declining. This narrowing of the difference is attributable to a greater decline in the regional rate.

By substituting population fourteen years of age and over for total population as the base and disaggregating participation by sex, a picture can be drawn of the relative rates of labor force participation by sex for the study period.

Participation rates for males declined both relatively and absolutely in the Region. The national male participation rate dropped absolutely; the decline which has taken place in the Mohawk Region was greater, and so the Region suffered a larger relative decline. Male participation fell from a higher than national rate in 1940 to a lower than national rate in 1960. A partial explanation for the relative decline may be attributed to the age structure of the Region's population — a greater than national per cent share of younger and older

45

Table B-31

Growth of Labor Force*
1960-1940

	Total Labor Force 1960	1940	Growth Rate of Labor Force 1940-1960 (Per cent)
Nation	69,877,481	53,010,582	1.4
New York	6,999,445	5,962,199	.8
Upstate	2,392,974	2,018,711	.9
Region	186,972	174,936	.3
SMSA	129,493	112,210	.7

* United States Bureau of the Census, *United States Census of Population 1960*, Vol. I, Pt. 1, Table 84; Pt. 34, Tables 52 and 83; *United States Census of Population 1940*, Vol. II, Pt. 3, Tables 16, 23, 33, and K41.

Table B-32

Labor Force Participation Rates*
1960, 1950, 1940

	(Per cent) 1960	1950	1940
Nation	39.0	39.9	40.1
New York	41.7	42.8	42.3
Upstate	39.3	40.8	41.4
Region	40.0	42.2	44.0
SMSA	39.1	40.8	42.6
	Concentration Coefficient		
Nation	1.000	1.000	1.000
Region	1.028	1.058	1.096

* United States Bureau of the Census, *United States Census of Population 1960*, Vol. I, Pt. 34, Tables 20, 73, and 83; Pt. 1, Table 83; *United States Census of Population 1950*, Vol. II, Pt. 32, Tables 35, 43, and 66; *United States Census of Population 1940*, Vol. II, Pt. 3, Tables 16, 23, 33, and K41.

persons — and to the fact that the region had a smaller than national share of males sixty-five years old and over in the labor force in 1960—28.9 per cent compared to 30.5 per cent. Female participation rates declined relatively during the twenty-year period, but still maintained an absolute increase. This was the result of rapid growth in female participation on the national level which acted to narrow the gap between the Mohawk Region rate and the United States rate.

Table B-33

Labor Force Participation Rates by Sex*
1960, 1950, 1940

	Males (Per cent)			Females (Per cent)		
	1960	1950	1940	1960	1950	1940
Nation	77.4	78.8	79.0	34.5	28.9	25.4
New York	78.1	78.6	77.1	37.0	32.3	32.0
Upstate	76.4	77.3	79.0	35.2	30.1	26.9
Region	75.8	77.9	79.1	37.4	32.9	30.8
SMSA	75.2	76.4	75.9	35.9	31.1	29.8
	Concentration Coefficient					
Nation	1.000	1.000	1.000	1.000	1.000	1.000
Region	.979	.989	1.001	1.081	1.138	1.213

* United States Bureau of the Census, *United States Census of Population 1960*, Vol. I, Pt. 34, Tables 20, 73, and 83; Pt. 1, Table 83; *United States Census of Population 1950*, Vol. II, Pt. 32, Tables 35, 43, and 66; *United States Census of Population 1940*, Vol. II, Pt. 3, Tables 16, 23, 33, and K41.

The role of women in the labor force increase of the Mohawk Region is most striking. For each of the ten-year periods, female entrants more than offset the losses produced by the decreasing male participation.

An examination of labor force growth rates — Tables B-34 and B-35 — provides a summation of significant relative and absolute changes in the regional labor force. The Region had an absolute increase in total labor force during the 1960-1940 period, but the rate of its growth was slower than in the nation. In the Mohawk Region, which started the period with a higher than national participation rate — Table B-32 — the relative difference in relation to the United States narrowed. Male participation decreased in the Region

Table B-34

Changes in the Level of Labor Force by Sex*
1960-1940

	Males	Females	Total	Per cent Females of Total
Nation	+7,344,355	+9,522,544	+16,866,899	56.5
Region	− 1,438	+ 13,474	+ 12,036	120.0

Decrease in Males	1940-1950	−141
	1950-1960	−1,297
Increase in Females	1940-1950	+2,950
	1950-1960	+10,524

* United States Bureau of the Census, *United States Census of Population 1960*, Vol. I, Pt. 34, Tables 20, 73, and 83; Pt. 1, Table 83; *United States Census of Population 1950*, Vol. II, Pt. 32, Tables 35, 43, and 66; *United States Census of Population 1940*, Vol. II, Pt. 3, Tables 16, 23, 33, and K41.

Table B-35

Labor Force Growth*
1960-1940

	Total Labor Force		Male L. F.		Female L. F.	
	Per cent Change	Rate of Growth	Per cent Change	Rate of Growth	Per cent Change	Rate of Growth
Nation	131.8	1.4	118.3	.8	173.9	2.8
Region	106.9	.3	−101.2	−.2	126.2	1.1

* United States Bureau of the Census, *United States Census of Population 1960*, Vol. I, Pt. 34, Tables 20, 73, and 83; Pt. 1, Table 83; *United States Census of Population 1950*, Vol. II, Pt. 32, Tables 35, 43, and 66; *United States Census of Population 1940*, Vol. II, Pt. 3, Tables 16, 23, 33, and K41.

both relatively and absolutely, while female participation declined only relatively in the Region. What occurred is that women constituted an increasing share of the Region's total labor force. Female entrants more than compensated for the loss caused by the decline in male participation, and entered the labor force at a rate sufficient to offset retiring males and account for *all* net additions to the regional labor force. It has been demonstrated previously that a major portion of female entrants are married women in families with husbands present.

Unemployment

Previous analysis established that the Mohawk Region continued to experience higher than national rates of labor force participation, and that the major reason for these high rates is attributable to relatively larger amounts of participation by females. Given high levels of labor force participation, it might be assumed, *a priori,* that the Mohawk Region has a higher number of employed income earners and hence a relatively higher total and participation income. This unfortunately does not necessarily prove to be the case, for statistics of labor force cannot be equated to and assumed to be statistics for employment. To arrive at employment estimates through the use of labor force data requires an adjustment for unemployment, and to generalize concerning incomes requires analysis of unemployment levels and structure along with other types of data such as weeks worked, hours worked, wages and salaries, employment structure, etc. These types of analyses will be carried out in other portions of this study; the emphasis here will be placed on an analysis of regional unemployment.

Level and Changes in Unemployment. Discussions of unemployment are most commonly carried on in terms of unemployment rates rather than in absolute numbers of unemployed. Using this measure, rates of unemployment for the Mohawk Region and the nation are presented in Table B-36, along with their concentration coefficients.[14]

Regional average total unemployment in 1960 was 7.5 per cent, a rate higher than that of either the nation or any other comparison area. When unemployment is broken down by sex, the rates of unemployment for both males and females are again higher for the Mohawk than the other areas.

Though there has been variation in the degree of deviation between regional and national rates, unemployment in the Mohawk Region remained consistently higher than in the nation. Each of the areas listed had significant decreases in its rates of unemployment between 1940 and 1960, though the actual declines may be overstated. Ques-

---

[14] Unemployment rates used in this study are established using civilian labor force as the base. The unemployment rate is the per cent of the civilian labor force unemployed.

tions of definitional discrepancy cast doubt on the 1940 statistics and hence their comparison with 1960 data, but it is still safe to assume that the drop in unemployment rates from 1940 to 1960 was significant.

Concentration Coefficient. Absolute levels of unemployment for 1960 are presented in Table B-36. Presentation in this form provides a more graphic picture of what unemployment rates signify with regard to job loss to persons.

The federal government has, in the past, taken issue with the great extent of emphasis the press has given to levels of unemployment and has suggested that attention also should be given to levels of employment. The argument is for giving at least as much public attention to positive aspects as to negative. Therefore, employment figures for the Mohawk Region are presented to provide a positive balance. A much lengthier discussion of regional employment will be presented in another section of this study.

Table B-36

Unemployment Rates by Sex*
1960, 1950, 1940

	1960 (Per Cent)		1950 (Per Cent)		1940 (Per Cent)	
	Male	Female	Male	Female	Male	Female
Nation	5.4	5.9	5.1	5.8	14.3	15.5
c.c.	(1.000)	(1.000)	(1.000)	(1.000)	(1.000)	(1.000)
New York	4.9	5.6	6.4	5.2	17.3	14.8
c.c.	(.907)	(.949)	(1.255)	(.897)	(1.210)	(.955)
Upstate	5.9	6.5	5.5	5.1	11.9	10.3
c.c.	(1.093)	(1.101)	(1.078)	(.879)	(.832)	(.665)
Region	7.1	8.1	7.2	6.3	14.3	11.4
c.c.	(1.315)	(1.373)	(1.412)	(1.086)	(1.000)	(.735)
SMSA	6.7	7.1	7.9	6.6	14.1	11.2
c.c.	(1.241)	(1.203)	(1.549)	(1.138)	(.986)	(.723)

* United States Bureau of the Census, *United States Census of Population 1960*, Vol. I, Pt. 34, Tables 27, 83, and 84; Pt. 1, Table 83; *United States Census of Population 1950*, Vol. II, Pt. 32, Tables 25, 35, and 43; *United States Census of Population 1940*, Vol. II, Pt. 32, Tables 38 and 39.

Table B-37

Absolute Unemployment by Sex and Total Labor Force*
1960

| | Unemployment | | |
	Male	Female	Total Labor Force
Nation (000)	2,563.3	1,322.1	69,877.5
New York (000)	225.2	134.6	6,999.4
Upstate (000)	94.6	51.4	2,393.0
Region (000)	8.7	5.3	187.0
SMSA (000)	5.8	3.1	129.5

* United States Bureau of the Census, *United States Census of Population 1960*, Vol. I, Pt. 1, Table 83; Pt. 34, Tables 27, 83, and 84.

Some 19.5 thousand more persons were employed in the Region in 1960 than in 1940. It is an addition to our knowledge of the Region to be able to distinguish whether this gain in employment is attributable to an increased number of persons in the labor force, or is the result of better utilization of a relatively constant size labor force. If employment has increased based on the first possibility, the increases are attributable to net increases in the size of the labor force; if attributable to the second, the increases in employment are the result of a more efficient use of a given-sized stock of labor resources, discounting skill factors.[15]

As indicated on Table B-39, increases in male employment for the Mohawk Region are attributable to a decrease in unemployment rather than changes in the size of the male labor force. Male labor force participation declined in the Region, but male unemployment rates have decreased more rapidly resulting in a greater absolute number of males employed. These changes in male employment and

---

[15] The method used for determining the reason for increased employment is as follows:
    (1) The original size of the labor force (1940)
    (2) minus the number of unemployed in the base year (1940)
    (3) plus the net change in the number employed (1960-1940)
    (4) plus the net change in labor force (1960-1940)
    (5) equals the actual employment in end year (1960)
The analysis was performed for male and female employment since it is reasonable that they may not have reacted similarly.

51

Table B-38

Employment Change in the Mohawk Region*
1960-1940

	Total Employed (000)	Males Employed (000)	Female Employed (000)
1940	151.0	105.9	45.1
1960	170.5	110.9	59.6
Increase 1940-1960	19.5	5.0	14.5

* United States Bureau of the Census, *United States Census of Population 1960*, Vol. I, Pt. 34, Table 83.

participation indicate that the Mohawk Region made more efficient use of its male labor force. For the nation, the greatest share of increases in male employment was due to increases in the size of the male labor force. National unemployment rates declined at the same time that there was an increase in male labor force participation.

Table B-39

Factors Contributing to Absolute Changes in Employment*
1960-1940

	Changes in Employment Due to Changes in Rate of Unemployment		Changes in Employment Due to Change in Labor Force Size	
	Male (000)	Female (000)	Male (000)	Female (000)
Nation	+3,411.7	+675.4	+7,344.4	+9,522.5
New York	+511.3	+117.7	+337.8	+699.5
Upstate	+79.6	+1.3	+138.9	+278.2
Region	+9.0	+1.6	−1.5	+13.4

* United States Bureau of the Census, *United States Census of Population 1960*, Vol. I, Pt. 34, Tables 20, 27, 73, 83, and 84; Pt. 1, Table 83; *United States Census of Population 1940*, Vol. II, Pt. 3, Tables 16, 23, 33 and K41; Pt. 32, Tables 38 and 39.

Increased female employment in the Region was the result of developments which are the reverse of those affecting male employment. Growth in female employment for the Region is attributable to the increases in the absolute size of the female labor force rather than to decreases in female unemployment. Women entered the regional labor force at a rate which was higher than the rate of decline in female unemployment. This same pattern of increased female employment was evident on the state and national levels, but was more pronounced in the Mohawk Region.

Data concerning the level and increases of total employment for the Region may present a picture which is more optimistic than is justified. Some distinction or recognition must be made between part-time and full-time employment. Table B-40 provides some indication of period of employment for the Region in relation to the State and nation.

Based on the data presented below, the Region had a higher per cent share of its employed labor force employed fifty to fifty-two weeks than did the nation, and hence the Region had a relatively smaller per cent of part-time employment.

Table B-40

Weeks of Employment of Those Working*
1959

| | Per Cent of Total Persons Employed in 1959 | | |
	Working 50-52 Weeks	Working 14-26 Weeks	Working 13 Weeks or Less
Nation	56.8	11.0	8.4
New York	60.6	7.7	8.8
Upstate	57.7	8.6	10.8
Region	58.6	8.4	9.2
SMSA	60.6	8.0	9.2

* United States Bureau of the Census, *United States Census of Population 1960,* Vol. I, Pt. 34, Tables 55, 76 and 86; Pt. 1, Table 85.

Skill Levels of the Unemployed. The level of unemployment depends upon the demand and supply of labor including the migration of labor. The unemployment mix — occupations of the unemployed — may have a composition similar to that of employed workers, or it may vary substantially. An illustration of the former case is that of coal miners where there is not sufficient demand to employ the labor available, though the unemployed have the same skills as those who are employed. An example of the latter is illustrated by an ex-agricultural worker in Princeton, New Jersey where the skills of the employed might be quite different from those of agricultural labor. Accepting this dichotomy and testing for it in the Mohawk Region provide some insight into the nature of regional unemployment and possible policies to alleviate the condition. If the skill levels of the unemployed and the employed do not vary significantly, it may be more rewarding to place less stress on changing the skill levels of the employed as a primary solution. Rather than placing primary emphasis on the supply side of the problem by attempting to vary the quality of available labor, more emphasis might be given to the demand side by attempting to change the industrial mix or promote labor migration to areas of job availability.

To gain information regarding the skill levels of the unemployed in the Mohawk Region, correlations were established between absolute employment and unemployment by occupation and sex. It was assumed that the occupation of an individual broadly defines his skill level, and that persons in the same occupation possess a relatively comparable level of skills. The analysis was disaggregated by sex to point up the possible differences which might exist between male and female unemployment and employment.

Table B-41

Correlations of Absolute Employment and Unemployment by Occupation and Sex*
1960

| | Coefficient (R) of Correlation | | Coefficient (R^2) of Determination | |
	Male	Female	Male	Female
Nation	.71	.76	.50	.57
New York	.74	.70	.55	.49
Region	.77	.84	.59	.71

* United States Bureau of the Census, *United States Census of Population 1960*, Vol. I, Pt. 34, Tables 60 and 85; Pt. 1, Tables 88 and 90.

Based on these correlations, the occupations of the unemployed in all three areas were significantly similar to those of the employed. This is particularly so for the Mohawk Region which displayed the strongest correlation.

Accepting the assumption of a normal distribution of skills within each occupation, the skill level of unemployed persons in the Mohawk Region does not differ significantly from those of the employed. Therefore, a simple supposition concerning the importance of raising skill levels cannot be assumed. It may still be desirable to raise skill levels if out-migration is considered desirable, but this is rarely stated as a policy goal. This is not intended as a recommendation against increasing skills, but is meant to indicate the importance of developing policies directed at the demand side of the unemployment problem.

Employment

The portions of the analysis of regional employment contained in this subsection are based on the data collected in the *United States Census of Population* and reflect employment by place of residence. This type of approach primarily reflects the supply aspect of employment in the Mohawk Region and measures the number of employed persons residing in the Region. The demand portion of the employment equation is primarily determined by the factors influencing the industrial structure of an area; such information is collected on the basis of place of employment rather than place of residence. The later type of data is primarily available in United States census volumes such as the *Census of Business* and the *Census of Manufacturing* as well as *County Business Patterns* and publications of the New York State Department of Labor. Analysis of employment on an establishment basis for the Mohawk Region will be presented in a later portion of this study. An attempt to reconcile the two types of employment data available for the Region will be made in a later chapter dealing with regional commuting.

Levels. Absolute employment figures are included to provide a clear picture of the actual magnitudes involved in the succeeding analysis and discussion. Too often, a discussion carried on in terms of rates and per cent changes remains somewhat abstract and removed, and makes it difficult to gauge the impact which change may have on the total population or labor force.

Table B-42

Employment Levels*
1960, 1950, 1940

	1960	1950	1940
Nation	64,639,247	56,435,273	45,070,306
New York	6,599,462	5,944,261	4,974,518
Upstate	2,226,822	3,038,799	1,692,624
Region	170,602	164,812	151,019
SMSA	118,205	106,796	97,316

* United States Bureau of the Census, *United States Census of Population 1960*, Vol. I, Pt. 1, Table 89; Pt. 34, Tables 84 and 120; *United States Census of Population 1950*, Vol. II, Pt. 32, Tables 28, 35, and 43; *United States Census of Population 1940*, Vol. II, Pt. 3, Tables 18, 23, 33, and K42.

Previous analysis established the significantly larger per cent share of female participation in the Mohawk Region's labor force. It is apparent from the data concerning employment that this higher percentage was reflected regionally in greater female employment.

For each of the years examined, the Mohawk Region had a higher per cent share of women employed than the nation. The pattern of female employment on a statewide basis had been quite similar to that displayed by the Region for the period under examination.

Previous analysis of labor force participation in the Mohawk Region indicated that the entire growth in regional labor force, 1940-1960, was attributable to increases in female participation since male participation suffered an absolute decline during the period. An examination of employment changes by sex for the same twenty-year period reveals that females accounted for only 74.1 per cent of the increase in total employment. The discrepancy between the hundred per cent contribution of females to increases in regional labor force and the seventy-four per cent contribution of females to increases in employment is the result of the decline in male unemployment which occurred between 1940 and 1960.

Rates of growth of both male and female employment for the Mohawk Region was slower than those of either the State or the nation. Relative growth of female to male employment followed the same pattern regionally as nationally, female employment growing more rapidly than male. Despite the fact that the regional growth

56

in female employment was slower than that of the nation, the employment of women was relatively more significant for the Region

Table B-43

Female Employment as a Per Cent of Total Employment*
1960, 1950, 1940

	1960 (Per Cent)	1950 (Per Cent)	1940 (Per Cent)
Nation	32.8	27.9	24.8
New York	34.4	31.0	29.2
Upstate	33.2	29.0	29.2
Region	34.9	30.9	29.9
SMSA	34.3	30.3	28.9

	Concentration Coefficient		
	1960	1950	1940
Nation	1.000	1.000	1.000
New York	1.049	1.111	1.178
Upstate	1.012	1.039	1.073
Region	1.064	1.108	1.206
SMSA	1.046	1.086	1.165

* United States Bureau of the Census, *United States Census of Population 1960*, Vol. I, Pt. 1, Table 89; Pt. 34, Tables 84 and 120; *United States Census of Population 1950*, Vol. II, Pt. 32, Tables 28, 35, and 43; *United States Census of Population 1940*, Vol. II, Pt. 3, Tables 18, 23, 33, and K42.

Table B-44

Changes in Employment Level*
1960-1940

	Rate of Growth				Absolute Change 1960-1940		Female Change
	1960-1950 (Per Cent)		1950-1940 (Per Cent)				Total Change (Per Cent)
	M	F	M	F	M	F	
Nation	.6	3.0	1.9	3.5	9,574,707	9,994,225	51.1
New York	.6	2.1	1.5	2.4	809,053	815,891	54.0
Upstate	.3	2.3	1.5	2.7	245,623	288,775	50.2
Region	.3	1.6	.8	1.2	5,057	14,466	74.1
SMSA	.4	2.3	.7	1.4	8,434	12,122	58.0

* United States Bureau of the Census, *United States Census of Population 1960*, Vol. I, Pt. 1, Table 89; Pt. 34, Tables 84 and 120; *United States Census of Population 1950*, Vol. II, Pt. 32, Tables 28, 35, and 43; *United States Census of Population 1940*, Vol. II, Pt. 3, Tables 18, 23, 33, and K42.

than the nation. This fact will be examined in more depth in the discussions of income and population migration.

Occupation. Having established the levels of both male and female employment and the growth of these levels between 1940 and 1960, it is important to attempt an analysis of the skill levels of the employed to determine if these changed significantly with the increases in employment. Data classifying employment by occupations provide an opportunity to gain partial insight into the nature of skill level changes which occurred in the Region. It must be cautioned, however, that the use of this data can provide only a partial approximation at best. Recognizing the difficulties inherent in the use of occupational categories, Table B-45 was constructed to estimate the per cent of increases in employment of persons in skilled occupations, including technical and professional occupations, managers, and craftsmen.

Table B-45

Per Cent Employed in Skilled Occupations by Sex*
1960, 1950, 1940

	1960 (Per Cent)		1950 (Per Cent)		1940 (Per Cent)	
	M	F	M	F	M	F
Nation	50.2	24.2	48.1	20.8	46.0	20.9
New York	49.2	25.0	46.2	20.0	41.1	19.2
Upstate	50.7	26.5	53.6	21.8	44.3	22.2
Region	48.8	23.6	42.6	19.9	39.1	18.0

* United States Bureau of the Census, *United States Census of Population 1960*, Vol. I, Pt. 1, Table 89; Pt. 34, Tables 84 and 120; *United States Census of Population 1950*, Vol. II, Pt. 32, Tables 28, 35, and 43; *United States Census of Population 1940*, Vol. II, Pt. 3, Tables 18, 23, 33, and K42.

The increases in the per cent of skilled persons employed in the Mohawk Region was significantly larger than that taking place for the nation as a whole: the per cent increase in the share of skilled employment was greater for females than males, and greater for the Region than the nation. Despite the increase experienced, the Region persisted in having higher levels of employment in unskilled and semi-skilled occupations than was evidenced by the other areas.

It is advisable once again to stress the limited reliability of this classification of skill levels and the need for closer examination of employment by occupation to establish employment patterns for the Region. This examination will be undertaken through the use of "shift analysis" to isolate changes in composition of employment by occupation which took place during the twenty-year period.[16]

Shift analysis attempts to analyze regional changes through the use of a more internally consistent national standard of change and isolate portions of regional change on the basis of stated standards. The tables and graphs presented below summarize the findings of a more detailed use of a shift analysis which were prepared for analytic purposes. The tables present total changes in employment by occupation and sex, while the graphs present a detailed picture of changes by occupation and sex.

The standard change represents the total change one would expect to have occurred in an area had that area experienced a per cent change similar to that of the nation and in each category contributing to the national total. Authors have used different titles to refer to these two components in the shift analysis — here they are titled national and functional changes, respectively — which together compose the standard for change. Thus, the standard measure is based on the actual total employment change for the nation, 1940-1950 and 1950-1960, adjusted for actual changes in the nation's occupational mix. The regional change in employment by occupation is measured against the national per cent changes in employment applied to the 1940 and 1950 regional base to arrive at the standard change for the Region. Actual regional change — the sum of actual 1940-1950 and 1950-1960 changes — is divided by the standard change to determine the per cent of the standard actually achieved by the Mohawk Region — which, in turn, provides a performance test for comparative purposes.

Male employment by occupation actually increased by 5,051 for the Region, a gain of only nineteen per cent of the standard.

---

[16] For a discussion of the shift analysis, see Edgar S. Dunn, Jr., "A Statistical and Analytical Technique for Regional Analysis," *Papers and Proceedings of the Regional Science Association*, VI (1960), pp. 101-14, and footnote 22 in the previous chapter.

Table B-46
Changes in Male Employment*
1960-1940

	Employment 1960	Employment 1940	Standard Change 1960-1940	Actual Change Standard Change (Per Cent)
Nation	43,466,946	33,892,239	9,574,707	100.0
New York	4,330,216	3,521,163	1,597,048	50.7
Upstate	1,487,933	1,242,510	450,372	54.5
Region	110,945	105,888	26,043	19.4
SMSA	77,628	69,194	19,547	43.1

* United States Bureau of the Census, *United States Census of Population 1960*, Vol. I, Pt. 1, Table 89; Pt. 34, Tables 84 and 120; *United States Census of Population 1950*, Vol. II, Pt. 32, Tables 28, 35, and 43; *United States Census of Population 1940*, Vol. II, Pt. 3, Tables 18, 23, 33, and K42.

Regional performance was substantially below that of either the State or upstate areas. The SMSA's performance was better than the Region as a whole — forty-three per cent — but still not as high as the other areas. It is obvious from the figures that those four counties of the Mohawk Region not included in the SMSA suffered an actual loss in male employment which was offset in the total regional figure by the gains registered in the SMSA. The total actual increase for the Region was 5,051; for the SMSA, 8,434.

The bar graphs included here are designed to illustrate the magnitudes of the changes which have occurred in male employment in the Region disaggregated by occupation. Where a cross-hatched segment of a bar exceeds the white segment, the actual regional share is above the standard. Reading from the graphs, total male employment in the Mohawk Region increased by some eight thousand between 1940 and 1950 whereas the standard gain was eighteen thousand. For the 1950-1960 period, the Region actually suffered a decrease of three thousand instead of a standard gain of nine thousand. In total, the Mohawk Region could have been expected to gain approximately twenty-eight thousand employed male residents between 1940 and 1960; in actual fact, it gained only some five thousand.[17]

---

[17] The different results indicated by the bar graphs and Table B-46 are the result of the use of different base periods.

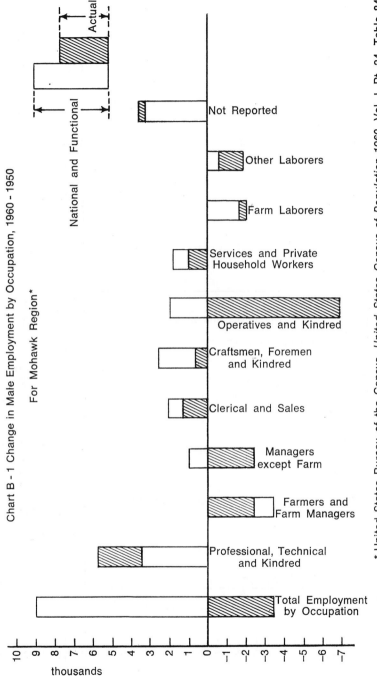

Chart B - 1 Change in Male Employment by Occupation, 1960 - 1950
For Mohawk Region*

National and Functional

Actual

Not Reported

Other Laborers

Farm Laborers

Services and Private Household Workers

Operatives and Kindred

Craftsmen, Foremen and Kindred

Clerical and Sales

Managers except Farm

Farmers and Farm Managers

Professional, Technical and Kindred

Total Employment by Occupation

thousands

* United States Bureau of the Census, *United States Census of Population 1960*, Vol. I, Pt. 34, Table 84; *United States Census of Population 1950*, Vol. II, Pt. 32, Table 35.

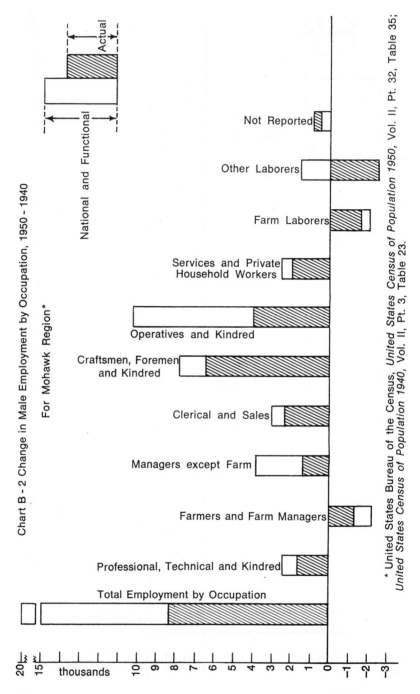

Chart B - 2 Change in Male Employment by Occupation, 1950 - 1940

For Mohawk Region*

National and Functional

Actual

Not Reported

Other Laborers

Farm Laborers

Services and Private
Household Workers

Operatives and Kindred

Craftsmen, Foremen
and Kindred

Clerical and Sales

Managers except Farm

Farmers and Farm Managers

Professional, Technical and Kindred

Total Employment by Occupation

20ᵏ
15ᵏ   thousands   10 9 8 7 6 5 4 3 2 1 0 -1 -2 -3

* United States Bureau of the Census, *United States Census of Population 1950*, Vol. II, Pt. 32, Table 35;
United States Census of Population 1940, Vol. II, Pt. 3, Table 23.

Employment of males in the professional, technical, and kindred category experienced the most notable gains in the Region for the 1940-50 and 1950-60 periods. Between 1950-60, regional growth in this category of employment was greater than the expected standard gain. Moderate gains were registered in other occupational categories, but none matched or bettered their standards.

Analysis of female employment by occupation is presented in the same form as that applied to males. Total figures are presented in tabular form, and disaggregated figures in the bar charts.

Table B-47

Changes in Female Employment *
1960-1940

	Employment 1960	Employment 1940	Standard Change 1960-1940	Actual Change Standard Change (Per Cent)
Nation	21,172,301	11,178,076	9,994,225	100.0
New York	2,269,246	1,453,355	1,238,820	65.9
Upstate	738,889	450,114	355,550	81.2
Region	59,657	45,131	34,452	42.0
SMSA	40,577	28,122	12,455	49.5

* United States Bureau of the Census, *United States Census of Population 1960,* Vol. I, Pt. 1, Table 89; Pt. 34, Tables 84 and 120; *United States Census of Population 1950,* Vol. II, Pt. 32, Tables 28, 35, and 43; *United States Census of Population 1940,* Vol. II, Pt. 3, Tables 18, 23, 33, and K42.

Increases in female employment in the Mohawk Region more closely approached the standard — forty-two per cent — than did male employment — nineteen per cent — a pattern similar to the State and upstate. Total actual increase in female employment for the Region numbered 14,526, while that for the SMSA was 12,455. This means that the four counties outside of the SMSA had a total increase of some 2,000 which again highlights the dominant role the SMSA plays in the regional economy.

The bar graphs illustrating female employment changes by occupation indicate the areas of greatest employment change. The greatest net gains in employment were registered in professional, technical, and kindred categories along with employment in clerical occupations.

63

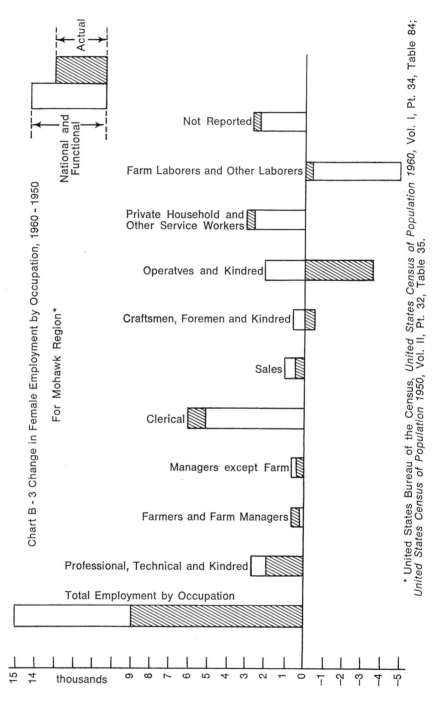

Chart B - 3 Change in Female Employment by Occupation, 1960 - 1950

For Mohawk Region*

National and Functional

Actual

Not Reported

Farm Laborers and Other Laborers

Private Household and Other Service Workers

Operatves and Kindred

Craftsmen, Foremen and Kindred

Sales

Clerical

Managers except Farm

Farmers and Farm Managers

Professional, Technical and Kindred

Total Employment by Occupation

15 14 thousands 9 8 7 6 5 4 3 2 1 0 -1 -2 -3 -4 -5

* United States Bureau of the Census, *United States Census of Population 1960*, Vol. I, Pt. 34, Table 84;
United States Census of Population 1950, Vol. II, Pt. 32, Table 35.

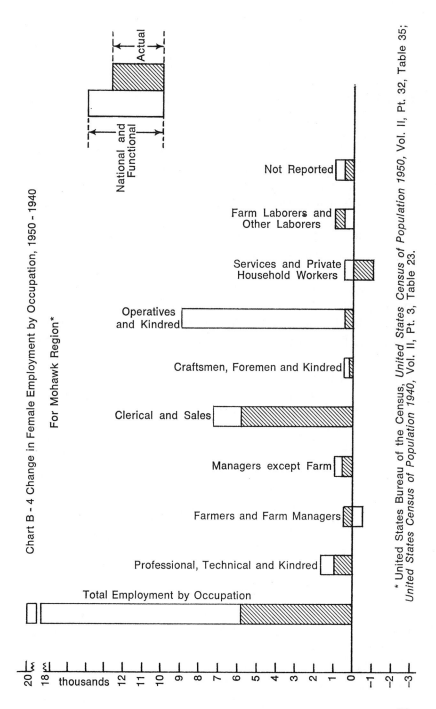

Chart B - 4 Change in Female Employment by Occupation, 1950 - 1940
For Mohawk Region*

National and Functional

Actual

Total Employment by Occupation

Professional, Technical and Kindred

Farmers and Farm Managers

Managers except Farm

Clerical and Sales

Craftsmen, Foremen and Kindred

Operatives and Kindred

Services and Private Household Workers

Farm Laborers and Other Laborers

Not Reported

thousands

20
18
12
11
10
9
8
7
6
5
4
3
2
1
0
-1
-2
-3

* United States Bureau of the Census, *United States Census of Population 1950*, Vol. II, Pt. 32, Table 35; *United States Census of Population 1940*, Vol. II, Pt. 3, Table 23.

During the 1950-1960 period, regional increases in clerical and service occupations were greater than expected standard increases. The number of females employed as operators and kindred declined absolutely during this same ten-year period. Gains in female employment in service occupations registered in the 1950-60 period were not sufficient to make up the losses suffered.

The sum of the functual share of the shift analysis provides information regarding the relative growth potential of the occupational mix. The functional share itself indicates the amount of standard change in employment in a particular functional category assuming the Region's and the nation's employment in the category changes at the same rate.

Table B-48 indicates that total male employment for the Mohawk Region had a negative functional share for 1940-1950 and a positive functional share for 1950-1960. Female employment displayed the reverse pattern: positive in 1940-1950 and negative in 1950-1960. On the basis of the evidence, males had an oucupational mix in 1940 which had increased nationally by 1950 at a rate of growth which was less than the growth for total employment — a negative relative growth occupational mix in 1950 and a positive relative growth occupational mix in 1960. An opposite situation prevailed for female employment. Thus, the change in the composition of occupational mix has become favorable for males and unfavorable for females. The high relative growth occupations became dominant for males during 1950-1960.

Table B-48

Functional Share of Total Employment by Occupation and Sex for the Mohawk Region *
1960-1940

	1960-1950	1950-1940
Male	+ 4,365	− 1,399
Female	− 1,361	+ 2,881

* United States Bureau of the Census, *United States Census of Population 1960*, Vol. I, Pt. 1, Table 89; Pt. 34, Tables 84 and 120; *United States Census of Population 1950*, Vol. II, Pt. 32; Tables 28, 35, and 43; *United States Census of Population 1940*, Vol. II, Pt. 3, Tables 18, 23, 33, and K42.

Industry. A summary of the employment mix by industry is presented in Table B-49 below. Per cent shares of total employment have been disaggregated by major industry classification.[18] Based on this breakdown, the Mohawk Region had a higher than national per cent share of its employment in the manufacturing and service and public administration industries. Employment in manufacturing played a greater role in total regional employment than it did for either the State or upstate.

Differential rates of growth between and among industries of the comparison areas are indicative of the changes in the structure of employment by industry which occurred during the twenty-year period.

These statistics present a clear indication of the slow rate of growth in industrial employment in the Mohawk Region compared to the national or state standards. Total employment increase during the twenty-year period was only 0.6 per cent for the Region, and this increase was more than accounted for by growth in the SMSA total.

Table B-49

Employment by Industry *
1960

	Total Employment	AFF	C&M	Mfg	TPUC	WRT	FIRE	SPA	NR
			Per Cent Share in Total Employment						
Nation	64,639,256	6.7	6.9	27.1	6.9	18.2	4.2	26.0	4.0
New York	6,598,462	1.8	5.1	28.6	7.7	18.2	6.2	27.1	5.3
Upstate	2,226,822	4.6	5.9	34.1	6.2	16.8	3.2	25.3	3.9
Region	170,542	5.7	4.8	36.5	4.8	15.1	3.1	26.3	3.7
SMSA	118,250	4.6	4.7	33.6	5.3	15.5	5.3	28.9	3.9

* United States Bureau of the Census, *United States Census of Population 1960*, Vol. I, Pt. 34, Tables 61, 75, and 85; Pt. I, Table 92.

---

[18] Industry classifications are as follows:

    AFF — Agriculture, Forestry, and Fisheries
    C&M — Construction and Mining
    Mfg — Manufacturing
  TPUC — Transportation, Public Utilities, and Communication
  WRT — Wholesale and Retail Trade
  FIRE — Finance, Insurance, and Real Estate
  SPA — Services and Public Administration
    NR — Not Reported

The four counties of the Region not included in the SMSA would have registered a net loss of some one thousand in employment for the 1960-1940 period if they were totaled alone. Agriculture was the only industry in the Region which experienced favorable employment changes when compared to the nation. This was true only because agricultural employment in the Mohawk Region has declined at a slower rate than for the nation as a whole. Employment growth in construction-mining, finance-insurance-and real estate, and services-public administration for the Mohawk Region was quite close to the growth rate in the nation. Manufacturing employment, the classification with the greatest per cent share of total employment in 1960, experienced negligible growth during the 1940-1960 period — less than .0105 per cent — and taken with the varying growth rates displayed by the other categories, it may be assumed that the Region may be developing an industrial employment mix similar to that of the nation.

Table B-50

Growth Rates of Employment by Industry*
1960-1940

	Absolute Change In Employment 1960-1940	Annual Growth Rate								
		Total	AFF	C&M	Mfg	TPUC	WRT	FIRE	SPA	NR
Nation	19,568,941	1.8	−3.4	2.0	2.5	1.7	2.3	3.0	2.5	6.6
New York	1,623,944	1.4	−3.0	1.4	2.3	1.0	0.3	1.6	1.4	5.8
Upstate	534,199	1.4	−3.2	2.3	3.3	0.5	−0.7	1.6	1.8	5.5
Region	19,523	0.6	−2.7	1.9	+	0.5	0.3	2.5	2.1	5.2
SMSA	20,889	1.0	−3.1	2.3	+	0.7	0.4	2.7	2.6	5.2

* United States Bureau of the Census, *United States Census of Population 1960*, Vol. I, Pt. 34, Tables 61, 75, and 85; Pt. 1, Table 92; *United States Census of Population 1940*, Vol. II, Pt. 3, Tables 18, 23, 33, and K42.

+ Indicates a value of less than 0.05.

Because of the relatively large absolute increase of female participation in the regional labor force, it is necessary to try to trace the changes which occurred in female industrial employment during the twenty-year period. A comparison of the growth rates of female employment presents information concerning changes in the composition of male employment as well.

Table B-51

Growth Rates of Female Industrial Employment*
1960-1940

	Total Change	Total	AFF	C&M	Mfg	TPUC	WRT	FIRE	SPA	NR
					Annual Growth Rate					
Nation	9,994,225	3.3	−0.9	7.0	3.2	4.1	5.1	2.4	6.8	3.9
New York	815,911	2.3	3.1	6.6	5.1	3.2	1.6	3.7	1.5	5.6
Upstate	288,776	2.5	7.8	6.8	0.2	5.3	0.8	5.1	1.9	5.5
Region	14,466	1.4	3.7	3.6	−0.3	4.5	2.3	5.0	2.0	5.3
SMSA	28,122	1.9	2.7	6.0	−0.1	5.3	4.9	2.5	2.4	5.0

* United States Bureau of the Census, *United States Census of Population 1960*, Vol. I, Pt. 34, Tables 61, 75, and 85; Pt. 1, Table 92; *United States Census of Population 1940*, Vol. II, Pt. 3, Tables 18, 23, 33, and K42.

Growth rates of female employment exceed rates of growth for male plus female employment in every industry category for the Mohawk Region except for manufacturing and services-public administration. What this means is that females became a larger part of total employment in a number of employment categories. This same type of change was evident at the national level, the difference being that female employment grew at faster rates than male employment in each category except finance-insurance-real-estate.

Using shift analysis to examine changes which occurred in the total level of regional employment produces the following conclusions. The Mohawk Region gained only thirty per cent of its standard increase in employment, while the State and upstate areas achieved fifty-seven per cent and fifty-two per cent respectively during the same period. Moreover, the negative value of the functional mix standard of the Mohawk Region indicated the regional mix of industries in the nation increased in employment at a lower rate than did total employment in the nation. Restated: The Mohawk Region was composed of relative slow-employment growth industries. In addition, taking the slow-growth nature of the region's industries into consideration, the Region was not able to maintain its share of employment in the slow-growth industries.

Table B-52

Shift in Total Industrial Employment*
1960-1940

	1960-1940 Change	Average National Standard	Functional Mix Standard	Regional Standard	Net Relative Change	Actual Standard Change (Per Cent)
Nation	20,996,834	20,996,834	——	——	—	100.0
New York	1,623,944	2,251,066	859,978	—1,444,853	—584,875	52.2
Upstate	534,199	769,535	165,698	—377,116	—211,418	57.1
Region	19,523	65,773	—3,005	—40,998	—44,003	31.1

* United States Department of Commerce, *Growth Patterns in Employment by County: 1940-1950 and 1950-1960*, Vol. II.

Disaggregation of industrial employment to include only the relative "growth" industries possessed by the Mohawk Region results in the inclusion of four industries. Growth industry here means that there has been higher relative employment increase in the industry regionally than nationally.

Two of these regional growth industries, agriculture and apparel, are declining industries for the nation, agriculture absolutely and apparel relatively. The two remaining industries, electrical machinery and public administration and armed forces, are increasing on the national level relative to total United States employment increases, and the Region is gaining a greater than national share of employment in these industries.

Table B-53

Regional Share of Employment Change*
1960-1940

	Agriculture	Apparel	Electrical and other Machinery	Public Administration and Armed Forces
New York	10,319	—116,223	33,036	—147,972
Region	1,082	2,508	4,686	6,361

* United States Department of Commerce, *Growth Patterns in Employment by County: 1940-1950 and 1950-1960*, Vol. II.

CHAPTER 3

Industry and Income in the Mohawk Valley

Analysis in Chapter Two established four employment growth sectors in the Region during the 1940-1960 period: agriculture, public administration, and two areas of manufacturing. This chapter will render a more detailed analysis of industrial employment and structure to isolate the major changes which occurred over time. Four sectors of the regional economy will be analyzed: agriculture; manufacturing; wholesale and retail trade and selected services; and government.

Industry

Disaggregation of industrial employment by county establishes the existence of relative and absolute employment growth industries. Table C-1 provides a summary of the various employment growth industries for the individual counties of the Mohawk Region.

Deviation of the regional industrial employment mix in 1960 from the national standard has been established by the use of concentration coefficients. The results of these standardizations are presented in Table C-2 below, disaggregated for each of the Region's counties. Regionally, there was a greater than standard employment in durable and non-durable manufacturing and in service industries. The structural changes which have occurred in the industrial mix between 1960 and 1940 will be analyzed in some detail in the sections which are to follow.

Agriculture: Industry and Employment

Historically, agriculture has played a significant role in the development of the Mohawk Region. The early development of dairy farming provided a strong basis for the industrialization which was to take

71

Table C-1

Summary Table of County Growth Industries*
1960-1950

	Large Employment With Both Absolute and Relative Growth	Large Employment With Relative But Not Absolute Growth	Large Employment With Absolute But Not Relative Growth
Fulton County	Apparel Electrical Machinery	Textiles Other Retail Misc. Mfg. Agriculture	Professional and Related Services Pub. Admin.
Hamilton County	Construction Other Retail	Lumber and Wood Products Hotels	Prof. and Rel. Services
Herkimer County	Electrical Machinery Public Admin.	Other Retail Misc. Mfg. Agriculture	Prof. and Rel. Services
Lewis County	Other Retail Pub. Admin.	Agriculture Misc. Mfg.	Prof. and Rel. Services
Montgomery County	Apparel	Agriculture Textiles Other Retail	Food and Kindred Electrical Machinery Misc. Mfg. Prof. and Rel. Services Pub. Admin.
Oneida County	Food and Kindred Motor Vehicles and Equipment Pub. Admin.	Agriculture Trucking and Warehousing	Textiles Other Retail F.I.R.E. Hotels and Private Services Prof. and Rel. Services

* United States Department of Commerce, *Growth Patterns in Employment by County: 1940-1950 and 1950-1960,* Vol. II.

Table C-2

Location Quotients of Employment by Industry*
1960

	AFF	C&M	Manufacturing		TPUC	WRT	FIRE	SPA	NR
			DUR	NON-DUR					
Nation	1.00	1.00	1.00	1.00	1.00	1.00	1.00	1.00	1.00
Region	.85	.70	1.14	1.86	.70	.83	.74	1.01	.93
Fulton	.46	.59	.47	2.44	.54	.77	.55	.72	1.05
Hamilton	.26	2.77	.39	.81	.56	.94	.79	1.27	1.52
Herkimer	1.18	.58	2.07	1.23	.58	.73	.64	.77	.47
Lewis	3.66	.88	.55	1.61	.39	.62	.45	.92	.55
Montgomery	1.16	.65	.63	2.89	.51	.83	.60	.77	.73
Oneida	.55	.71	1.43	.70	.83	.94	.88	1.20	1.10
SMSA	.69	.68	1.33	1.13	.77	.85	.83	1.11	.97

* United States Bureau of the Census, *United States Census of Population 1960*, Vol. 1, Pt. 34, Tables 61, 75 and 85; Part 1, Table 92.

place. The emergence of the leather industry in Fulton County and the latter development of the food processing industry in the Mohawk Region counted heavily on the agriculture of the surrounding area. Three of the Region's six counties had greater per cent shares of employment in agriculture in 1960 than did the nation as a whole.

Since the number of farms is decreasing, and the size of farms is increasing at a rate less than the decrease in the number of farms, and the total sales of all farms are increasing faster than the acreage per farm, then the sales per farm must be rising. In like fashion, sales per acre also must have been growing since total acreage in farms shrunk. Because the number of farms decreased, sales per farm in 1959 were greater than in 1940.

The change in the location of the modal class of farms — an increase from $1,000-2,499 to $10-19,999 — is a reflection of the changes described along with increases in the price level exhibited for farm products. The modal class of farm sales is lower for Fulton than for the other counties of the Region.

Average value per farm and per acre are greatest in Oneida County, but the largest growth in these values during the nineteen-year period took place in Fulton County, another reflection of the rapid drop which occurred in the number of farms and the smaller drop in total acreage.

Table C-3

Selected Characteristics of Farms*
1959-1940

	1959 Number of Farms	1940-1959 Growth Rate in Number of Farms (Per Cent)	1959 Size of Farms (Average Acres)	1940-1959 Growth Rate of Size (Per Cent)	1959 Proportion of Area in Farms (Per Cent)	1940 Proportion of Area in Farms (Per Cent)
Nation (000)	3,711	—2.7	303	2.9	———	——
Region	6,860	—3.2	175	2.0	29.2	46.6
Fulton	591	—4.3	136	2.2	25.2	37.5
Hamilton	40	—10.1	122	—0.4	0.5	2.9
Herkimer	1,383	—2.7	164	1.4	28.3	31.7
Lewis	1,291	—2.7	225	1.8	35.1	41.1
Montgomery	1,974	—2.8	179	2.3	73.4	80.0
Oneida	2,511	—3.4	163	2.1	52.1	65.2
SMSA	3,894	—3.2	163	1.9	39.2	47.1

* United States Bureau of the Census, *United States Census of Agriculture 1959*, Vol. I, Pt. 7, Tables 1, 3, and 5; Vol. II, Chap. 1, Table 9; *United States Census of Agriculture 1945*, Vol. I, Pt. 2, Tables 1, 5, and 7; Vol. II, Chap. 1, Table 8.

Table C-4

Selected Data on Farm Output in Region*
1959-1940

	Per Cent Dairy Farms 1959	1940	Sale of Dairy Products Per Cent of All Products Sold—1959	Rate of Growth in Sales 1940-59	1940-1959 Rate of Growth of All Farm Products Sold	Commercial Farms, Value of Products Sold, Modal Class of Farm 1959 (000)	1940 (000)
Fulton	44.4	44.4	70.9	7.0	6.1	$5-10	$1-2.5
Hamilton	0.0	6.7	N.A.	N.A.	—4.0	N.A.	1-2.5
Herkimer	74.3	68.3	78.9	8.1	6.6	10-20	1-2.5
Lewis	73.3	76.3	78.9	7.0	7.4	10-20	1-2.5
Montgomery	77.4	67.8	83.8	7.7	7.3	10-20	1-2.5
Oneida	60.8	59.5	72.1	7.0	5.9	10-20	1-2.5
SMSA	65.6	62.4	75.8	7.0	6.5	10-20	1-2.5

* United States Bureau of the Census, *United States Census of Agriculture 1959*, Vol. I, Pt. 7, Tables 1, 5, and 6; *United States Census of Agriculture 1945*, Vol. I, Pt. 2, Tables 1, 4, 5, and 7.

Subtraction of the expenditures made per farm from the value of total sales per farm provides an approximate figure of gross proprietory income. Based on the information available, Montgomery County had the highest gross proprietary income per farm in 1959. It is possible, by establishing gross proprietary income per value of farm — land and buildings per farm — to estimate the gross or total profit rate per farm for each of the five counties in the Mohawk Region having a significant agricultural industry. Using this measure of profit, agriculture in Lewis County provided the greatest gross profit return in 1959 — 27.7 per cent. It must be cautioned that this measure does not reflect investments in livestock or certain other farm in-puts which are important in dairy farming, nor does it reflect the returns received from the sales of farm land.

Table C-5

Selected Data on Farm Value in Region*
1959-1940

| | 1959 Aver. Value of Land and Buildings | | 1940-1959 Growth Rate in Value of Land and Buildings | | Commercial Farms, 1959 Sales Minus Expenditures (including labor) | | |
	Per Farm	Per Acre	Per Farm (Per Cent)	Per Acre	Total (000)	Per Farm	Per Value of Land & Buildings on Farm (Per Cent)
Fulton	$18,501	$133	8.6	6.1	$ 150	$4,453	23.2
Hamilton	7,333	60	1.8	2.2	N.A.	N.A.	N.A.
Herkimer	19,514	96	7.2	4.7	4,726	4,258	10.4
Lewis	14,663	64	5.5	3.5	4,557	4,521	27.7
Montgomery	22,304	129	7.3	5.0	4,170	4,577	18.2
Oneida	23,238	141	8.3	6.0	6,755	3,763	13.9
SMSA	21,915	125	7.9	5.5	11,481	3,952	18.0

* United States Bureau of the Census, *United States Census of Agriculture 1959*, Vol. I, Pt. 7, Tables 1 and 57; *United States Census of Agriculture 1945*, Vol. I, Pt. 2, Tables 1 and 4.

Manufacturing by Establishment

Manufacturing data, collected on an establishment basis, indicate the magnitude of manufacturing activity actually taking place within the Mohawk Region. In terms of employment, these data approximate the number of persons employed in manufacturing firms in the Region, though the employees themselves may or may not reside in the Region.

Previous discussions of manufacturing employment in Chapter Two included only residents of the Region employed in manufacturing though they could reside in the Region and commute out of the Region. As can be expected, these two types of data, one collected on the basis of establishment and the other on the basis of residence, do not correspond, and need to be reconciled. An attempt at reconciliation is made in the discussion of regional commuting in Chapter Four.

Table C-6

Employment and Value Added by Manufacturing*
1963-1947

| | Employment | | Value Added (000) | | Region as Per Cent of New York | |
	New York	Region	New York	Region	Employ.	V.A.
1947	1,775,975	77,179	9,666,588	352,852	4.3	3.7
1954	1,896,000	63,358	14,140,524	453,530	3.3	3.2
1958	1,915,877	59,015	15,892,629	471,088	3.1	3.0
1963	1,853,050	56,997	19,559,120	592,482	3.1	3.0

* United States Bureau of the Census, *United States Census of Manufacturers 1947*, Vol. III, Table 2; *United States Census of Manufacturers 1958*, Vol. III, Table 3; *United States Census of Manufacturers 1963: Area Statistics*, Table 4.

The regional share of state employment in manufacturing and value added by manufacture decreased between 1947 and 1963, with the bulk of the decrease taking place between 1947 and 1954. In absolute terms, manufacturing employment in the Mohawk Region declined by some twenty thousand for the sixteen-year period. At the same time, the State was experiencing an increase of seventy-seven thousand. Seventy per cent of the Region's employment decline occurred between 1947 and 1954, a reflection of the cooling-off of high wartime employment and the cessation of the immediate post-war boom. Unfortunately for the consistency of data, the census of 1947 was taken during the post-war boom period, while the 1954 census was taken during a general recession. Therefore, it is quite probable that regional employment levels tended to fluctuate significantly during the period, but it is evident that the total employment losses in manufacturing suffered during the 1947-1954 period were never recouped, and that the trend continued through 1963. Based

Table C-7

Selected Characteristics of Manufacturing Establishments *
1963-1947

	1963 Number of Establishments	1963-1947 Growth Rate in Number of Establishments (Per Cent)	1963 Total Manufacturing Employment	1963-1947 Growth Rate of Employment (Per Cent)	1963 Average Employment per Establishment	1963 Production Workers (Per Cent)	1963-1947 Growth Rate of Production Worker (Per Cent)
Nation	311,784	1.6	16,598,000	1.1	54	72	.2
New York	47,041	—.1	1,853,050	.3	39	67	—.8
Region	882	—.1	56,997	—1.9	65	74	—1.1
Fulton	227	—2.3	8,312	—1.7	37	86	—1.0
Hamilton	18	3.1	108	—1.8	6	87	—1.2
Herkimer	119	1.9	11,909	—1.4	100	75	—.4
Lewis	52	2.7	1,883	.4	36	75	1.3
Montgomery	112	.7	8,220	—3.3	73	75	—2.7
Oneida	354	.2	26,565	—2.0	75	69	—1.0
SMSA	473	.6	38,474	—1.8	81	71	—.8

* United States Bureau of the Census, *United States Census of Manufacturers 1947*, Vol. III, Table 2; Vol. I, Chap. 1, Table 2; *United States Census of Manufacturers 1958*, Vol. III, Table 3; *United States Census of Manufacturers 1963: Area Statistics*, Table 4; *Summary Statistics: General Summary*, Table 3.

on available data, the Region appeared to be maintaining a constant portion of total state manufacturing employment since 1954.

Regional per cent share of value added by manufactures followed a trend similar to that for the regional share of state employment: a decline from wartime and post-war booms, and a leveling off to a constant three per cent share. Absolute levels of regional value added did not suffer the decline experienced by regional employment, but increased to a lesser extent than did value added for the State as a whole. Value added by manufacturers in the Mohawk Region experienced a 169 per cent increase for the 1947-1963 period compared to a 201 per cent increase for the State. Decline in regional per cent share is a result of this relatively smaller per cent increase.

Contrary to the national trend, the Mohawk Region and the State experienced a decline in the number of manufacturing establishments in the 1947-1963 period. In only two of the Region's counties, Hamilton and Lewis, was the growth rate in number of establishments greater than in the nation. Neither county, however, can be considered as a heavy manufacturing area. The absolute increases in the number of establishments for Hamilton and Lewis Counties were seven and eighteen respectively. For the Region, the number of establishments increased relative to manufacturing employment and production workers — this relationship held for each county except Fulton — thus average establishment size is decreasing.

Total manufacturing employment decreased for the Region, and for each of its counties except Lewis. The regional trend ran counter to both the state and national trend. Montgomery County experienced the greatest relative decrease in manufacturing employment during the 1947-1963 period.

The average employment size of manufacturing firms was larger for the Mohawk Region than for the nation as a whole, but given the existent relationship between the growth in number of establishments and growth of production workers both regionally and nationally, this difference should diminish over time. The Region and the bulk of its counties also displayed a higher than standard per cent share of production workers to all employees. In the Region and each of its six counties, growth of production workers was declining less rapidly than the decrease in total manufacturing employment, indicating a decline in the number of non-production workers in manufacturing industries in the Mohawk Region.

78

Productivity. Despite the wide usage of the term productivity, there is considerable disparity regarding its actual formulation and meaning as an economic concept. The productivity measure used in this study has been constructed from available data: value added and total employment in manufacturing.

Table C-8

Growth in Value Added, Employment, and Productivity *
1963-1947

	Growth Rates in Value Added (Per Cent)	Growth Rates in Employment (Per Cent)	Increase in Productivity (Per Cent)	Relative Productivity† (Per Cent)
Nation	6.1	1.1	5.0	....
New York	4.5	.3	4.2	—.8
Region	3.3	—1.9	5.2	.2
Fulton	2.4	—1.7	4.1	—.9
Hamilton	.6	—1.8	2.4	—2.6
Herkimer	6.8	—1.4	8.2	3.2
Lewis	3.0	.4	2.6	—2.4
Montgomery	+**	—3.3	3.3	—1.7
Oneida	3.0	—2.0	5.0	0.0
SMSA	4.2	—1.8	6.0	1.0

* Derived from United States Bureau of the Census, *United States Census of Manufacturers 1947*, Vol. III, Table 2; *United States Census of Manufacturers 1958*, Vol. III, Table 3; *United States Census of Manufacturers 1963: Area Statistics*, Table 4.
** Less than 0.1 per cent
† Computed by subtracting average United States productivity from area productivity.

The Mohawk Region and each of its six counties had positive increases in productivity between 1947-1963, but in only one case was relative productivity positive. Herkimer County experienced growth of sufficient magnitude to provide the Region with a positive growth total. Productivity increases for the Region were the result of growth in manufacturing output accompanied by decreases in the number of employees in manufacturing. One exception to this pattern took place in Lewis County, the only county which experienced positive growth in employment 1947-1963. For Montgomery County, the entire attributable increase in productivity resulted from a decline in employment rather than any increase in output; *i.e.,* it took fewer people to produce the same output.

Capital and Returns. Absolute levels of new capital per employee for the Region in both 1954 and 1963 were significantly below United States standard.[1] Despite the greater per cent increase in per employee new capital experienced by the Mohawk Region during this period, the absolute difference between the Region and the nation widened. Only two counties, Lewis and Hamilton, showed higher than national increments for either or both 1954 and 1963, and neither could be considered as being heavily engaged in manufacturing. It was established previously that both counties were primarily rural, and Lewis heavily agricultural in nature. What is indicated is that the manufacturing which did exist in these areas tended to be capital intensive.

Table C-9

New Capital Expenditures*
1963-1954

	Per Employee		Per Cent Increase 1963-1954	Growth Rates of Total New Capital 1963-1954 (Per Cent)
	1954	1963		
Nation	$485	$652	34.4	3.9
New York	302	423	40.1	3.6
Region	236	388	64.4	4.4
Fulton	134	131	—2.2	1.1
Hamilton	400	1,074	168.5	2.1
Herkimer	189	421	122.8	8.7
Lewis	621	1,067	71.8	6.9
Montgomery	240	392	63.3	2.6
Oneida	257	401	56.0	3.5
SMSA	237	407	71.7	4.9

* United States Bureau of the Census, *United States Census of Manufacturers 1954,* Vol. III, Table 3; Vol. I, Chap. 1, Table 2A; *United States Census of Manufacturers 1963: Area Statistics,* Table 4; *Summary Statistics: General Summary,* Table 3.

---

[1] The capital being analyzed is the gross addition, or increment to capital, added in a year. This is a gross figure because of the inclusion of replacements for depreciated, damaged, and destroyed capital.

80

Analysis of the growth rates of total new capital expenditures, rather than per employee expenditures, provides a somewhat different picture of regional development. Regional growth was greater than national standard, but this was a reflection of high capital expenditure growth in two counties — Herkimer and Lewis. Capital expenditure growth in both counties was significantly higher than United States growth, and in the case of Herkimer County, the capital expenditure growth has brought per employee capital expenditures close to national standard.

In an attempt to better understand the basic economic changes which occurred and are occurring in the manufacturing sector of the regional economy, it was believed desirable to develop data pertaining to the rate of return on capital invested in manufacturing. In developing this data, the authors concluded that return on new capital was a factor of prime importance to a potential investor in new plant and equipment, and it was this return which we set about deriving.

The rates of return which were developed are neither for total capital nor for net investment, but for new capital added. These rates present returns to gross increments to capital; data limitations pre-

Table C-10

Gross Proprietary Income*
1963-1954

	GPI 1954 (000)	GPI 1963 (000)	Changes in GPI 1963-1954 (000)
Nation	$54,070,000	$90,595,000	$36,525,000
New York	6,407,000	8,269,000	1,862,000
Region	218,982	294,047	75,065
Fulton	12,291	22,033	9,742
Hamilton	527	312	−215
Herkimer	47,822	110,738	62,916
Lewis	6,515	5,280	−1,235
Montgomery	39,636	37,917	−1,719
Oneida	112,191	117,767	5,576
SMSA	160,013	228,505	68,492

* United States Bureau of the Census, *United States Census of Manufacturers 1954*, Vol. III, Table 3; Vol. I, Chap. 1, Table 2A; *United States Census of Manufacturers 1963: Area Statistics*, Table 4; *Summary Statistics: General Summary*, Table 3.

vent the establishment of returns to net capital increments, or to total capital stock.

The first step used in establishing returns to new capital was to determine Gross Proprietary Income (GPI) which was taken to be the difference between value added and total payroll in manufacturing. Gross Proprietary Income is the total residual, including depreciation, available to the owners of manufacturing establishments.

Having derived GPI for the 1954-1963 period, the next and final step required a division by the average increase in new capital 1954-1963. The calculation described above is the marginal rate of return on gross investment in the period 1954-1963.

Table C-11

Rate of Return on New Capital *
1963-1954

	Change of GPI (1) (000)	Average Increase of New Capital (2) (000)	Marginal Rate of Return on Gross Investment (1) ÷ (2) (Per Cent)	Rank
Nation	$36,525,000	$9,607,204	3.8	—
New York	1,862,000	677,840	2.8	—
Region	75,065	18,537	4.1	—
Fulton	9,742	1,064	9.2	2
Hamilton	—215	106	—2.0	4
Herkimer	62,916	3,688	17.1	1
Lewis	—1,235	1,554	—8.0	6
Montgomery	—1,719	2,887	—6.0	5
Oneida	5,576	9,237	.6	3
SMSA	68,492	12,925	5.3	—

* United States Bureau of the Census, *United States Census of Manufacturers 1954*, Vol. III, Table 3; Vol. I, Chap. 1, Table 2A; *United States Census of Manufacturers 1963: Area Statistics,* Table 4; *Summary Statistics: General Summary,* Table 3.

Viewing these figures as relative measures of the increase in returns to new capital, the Mohawk Region in total experienced an increase in rate of return to new capital in manufacturing, and hence, compared to a national increase of a positive 3.8 per cent, appeared to offer a greater inducement for continued capital investment. In the county breakdown, Fulton and Herkimer experienced greater than national increases in returns but, as can be witnessed from the data, the economic conditions in these two counties varied greatly. Fulton County had the slowest growth in new capital expenditures while Herkimer had the largest. Coupled with the data on the increase of GPI, it would appear that the GPI increase in Herkimer County stimulated a high level of new investment, whether gross or net is impossible to say, while Fulton County's increased GPI occurred with only a small increase in the level of new capital investment, and quite probably, in a framework of disinvestment. For each of the other four counties, increase of new capital took place at a greater rate than increases in GPI, resulting in a negative increase in rates of return on new capital.

Table C-12

Selected Characteristics of Manufacturers *
1963-1947

	(1) Payroll All Employees 1963	(2) Total Wages Production Workers 1963	(3) (2) ÷ (1) (Per Cent)	(4) Value Added Per Employee 1963	1963-1947 Growth Rates For Columns		
					(1)	(2)	(4)
						(Per Cent)	
Nation	$5,868	$5,067	86.3	$11,227	4.8	4.4	4.9
New York	6,093	4,939	81.1	10,555	4.6	3.9	4.2
Region	5,236	4,509	86.1	10,395	4.4	3.9	5.3
Fulton	3,926	3,470	88.4	6,577	4.1	3.9	4.1
Hamilton	4,241	4,468	105.4	7,130	3.8	4.0	2.2
Herkimer	5,329	4,714	88.5	14,628	4.5	4.0	7.8
Lewis	5,334	4,605	86.3	8,138	4.6	4.4	2.5
Montgomery	4,451	3,844	86.4	9,064	3.4	2.8	3.4
Oneida	5,844	5,020	85.9	10,277	4.7	4.2	4.9
SMSA	5,685	4,919	86.5	11,624	4.6	4.1	6.0

* United States Bureau of the Census, *United States Census of Manufacturers 1947*, Vol. III, Table 2; Vol. I, Chap. 1, Table 2; *United States Census of Manufacturers 1958*, Vol. III, Table 3; *United States Census of Manufacturers 1963: Area Statistics*, Table 4; *Summary Statistics: General Summary*, Table 3.

The ratio of wages per production worker to payroll per employee differed little between the Region and the nation. Estimates of value added per employee emphasize the importance of the SMSA counties in the total manufacturing of the Region. Oneida and Herkimer Counties had the largest value added of the six counties.

Growth rates of value added per employee — productivity — were higher than the United States rate for the Region, but only because of the high performance of Herkimer County and the standard performance of Oneida County. Each of the other four counties performed at less than the national rate. Growth of payroll per employee has been lower for the Region than the nation, as has been the growth rate of total wages.

Average payroll per employee and wage per production worker were lower in the Mohawk Region than they were on the national level. For both measures, the regional average was some eighty-nine per cent of the national figure. Not one of the regional averages matched or surpassed the national average totals. Averages for Fulton County compare least favorably with national standard in both columns.

Regional manufacturing employment tends to be concentrated in a relatively small number of industries. In 1958, five manufacturing industries provided forty-nine per cent of total manufacturing employment for the Region. By 1963, employment in these five industries — food and kindred, textile mill products, leather and leather products, primary metals, and machinery, except electrical — had decreased to forty-six per cent of the total. In 1963, also an additional eleven per cent of the Region's manufacturing employees were employed in the manufacture of electrical machinery, but due to disclosure problems it is not possible to make comparisons for earlier years. This means fifty-eight per cent of regional manufacturing employment in 1963 was in six manufacturing categories.[2]

Table C-13 presents summary data on manufacturing employment by industry group, and indicates the major changes which took place between 1958 and 1963. From the available data, it can be broadly determined that only four of thirteen industrial categories experienced positive increases in employment. If the information was available, it may well be that electrical machinery would prove to have had the greatest employment increase regionally. Otherwise, according to the Table C-13, paper and related products experienced the greatest absolute and per cent increase.

---

[2] This figure is most probably an underestimate, for regional totals were arrived at through the aggregation of county data, and county employment totals may not have been presented because of the United States census disclosure policies.

Table C-13

Regional Employment by Major Manufacturing Sector *
1963-1958

S.I.C.**	Employment 1958	Employment 1963	Per Cent Change 1958-1963	S.I.C.	Employment 1958	Employment 1963	Per Cent Change 1958-1963
Total	58,843	56,997	—3.1	31	6.638	7,399	11.5
	100.0%	100.0%			11.3%	13.0%	
20	3,704	3,313	—15.5	33	6,282	5,154	—18.0
	6.3%	5.8%			10.7%	9.0%	
22	6,638	4,347	—35.5	34	3,249	2,442	—24.8
	11.3%	7.6%			5.5%	4.3%	
23	2,981	3,893	30.6	35	5,464	6,290	15.1
	5.1%	6.8%			9.3%	11.0%	
24	589	475	—19.4	36	(D)***	6,358	(D)
	1.0%	.8%				11.2%	
25	1,038	465	—7.0	37	2,734	2,095	—24.4
	1.8%	1.7%			4.7%	3.7%	
26	2,060	2,437	27.5	NR	17,476	10,923	
	2.4%	4.3%					
27	848	906	6.8				
	1.4%	1.6%					

* United States Bureau of the Census, *United States Census of Manufacturers 1958,* Vol. III, Tables 5 and 6; *United States Census of Manufacturers: Area Statistics,* Tables 6 and 7.

** Standard Industrial Classification:
- 20 Food & Kindred
- 22 Textile Mill Products
- 23 Apparel & Related
- 24 Lumber & Wood Products
- 25 Furniture & Fixtures
- 26 Paper & Related Products
- 27 Printing & Publishing
- 31 Leather & Leather Products
- 33 Primary Metal Industries
- 34 Fabricated Metal Products
- 35 Machinery, Except Electrical
- 36 Electrical Machinery
- 37 Transportation Equipment

*** No information due to disclosure rule.

While total manufacturing employment had a -3.1 per cent change, compared to a national per cent change of 5.8 per cent, a number of manufacturing sectors experienced considerably greater negative changes. The largest absolute and percentage employment loss has occurred for textile mill products, 2,300 employees or a -35 per cent. Large percentage losses, twenty-five per cent or more, have been

line 6. Omit "five" from "twenty-five"

registered in the fabricated metals and transportation equipment sectors.

Retail and Wholesale Trade, and Selected Services

Information summarizing trade and service activities in the Mohawk Region are presented by major sector and compared to state averages in Table C-14. General trends in regional activities followed those experienced by the State fairly closely, and where deviations have occurred, they have tended to narrow the absolute gap between the Region and the State to make the Region appear more similar to state averages.

Growth of total number of wholesale establishments was the only case in which regional performance was the reverse of statewide activity: positive growth in the Region and negative growth for the State. Wholesale establishments increased in payroll per employee for both areas, with a slightly greater growth regionally than statewide.

Sales per establishment by retail trade and selected services were lower on a regional than on a state basis. Comparing growth rates

Table C-14

Business Activity *
1963-1948

	Growth Rate in Number of Establishments 1963-1948 (Per cent)	Sales Per Est. 1963 (000)	Growth Rate Sales/est. 1963-1948 (Per cent)	Employment Per Est. 1963	Growth Rate Empl./est. 1963-1948 (Per cent)	Payroll Per Employee 1963 (000)	Growth Rate Payroll/Empl. 1963-1948 (Per cent)
Retail Trade							
New York	—1.2	$146	4.6	7.5	4.4	3.5	2.8
Region	—1.3	114	4.6	5.8	4.7	3.2	3.5
Wholesale Trade							
New York	—0.6	$1,649	3.3	10.3	1.5	10.3	6.2
Region	.1	733	3.7	8.3	.6	8.3	7.0
Selected Services							
New York	2.2	$ 84	6.8	9.0	8.1	4.6	3.9
Region	3.8	27	6.2	5.1	8.6	3.6	1.4

* United States Bureau of the Census, *United States Census of Business 1963: Retail Trade: New York,* Tables 5 and 8; *Wholesale Trades New York,* Tables 5 and 8; *Selected Services: New York,* Table 3; *United States Census of Business 1948,* Vol. II, Table 104; Vol. V, Table 103; *United States Census of Business 1947,* Table 103a.

of sales per establishment reveals that only regional wholesale trade experienced growth greater than the state average, but here again, this only served to raise the absolute level of regional activity closer to the state level. Growth in sales per service establishment was relatively greater than in the wholesale and retail trade sectors. Total retail and wholesale trade and services receipts were growing more rapidly than average incomes for both the Region and the State. Increases in employment per establishment varied between sectors with greater than standard increases experienced in retail and service sectors and less than standard increase in wholesale.

In no instance was absolute payroll per employee higher regionally than for New York State despite greater regional growth in the trade sectors during the period. For both trade sectors, regional averages were converging towards the state rate, but the gap between the averages for selected services, regional to state, was widening.

Comparative Analysis of Governmental Revenues and Expenditures

The total number of governmental units in the Mohawk Region declined from 392 in 1957 to 330 in 1962. Any attempt at a detailed discussion of the revenues and expenditures of this large number of governments would lead to a host of partial and incomplete conclusions of doubtful utility. Therefore, it was decided that a general fiscal comparison of the Mohawk Region's 330 governments is necessary if conclusions regarding the region's public sector are to be made useful and readily understandable. In presenting such a comparison, the discussion will be separated into two parts: first, a share analysis of revenues and expenditures by type of government; and secondly, a summary discussion of regional trends in local fiscal policies.

Examination of available data indicates that various types of governments — county, large city and villages, special district and other — tend to differ greatly in the scope and direction of their activities. The tables below are constructed to highlight the differences between these governments in their level and type of revenues and expenditures and the trends in their activities.

As indicated, special district and "Other" governments are most significant in terms of absolute level of revenues and expenditures. Other governments — school districts and other special districts plus town and small village local governments — had nearly sixty per

Table C-15

Mohawk Region Local Government
Total Revenues and Expenditures *
1962

Region Governments	Revenues (000)	Per cent	Expenditures (000)	Per cent
County	$31,586	25.8	$31,569	25.6
Large City or Village	18,095	14.8	17,352	14.0
Other	72,634	59.4	74,625	60.4
Total	122,315	100.0	123,546	100.0

* United States Bureau of the Census, *United States Census of Governments 1962*, Vol. VII, No. 32, Tables 32-34.

Table C-16

Mohawk Region Local Governments
Total Revenue by Type *
1962

Region Governments	Revenue Own Sources (000)	Inter-governmental Revenue (000)	Total General Revenue (000)
County	$16,322 (13.3)**	$15,264 (12.5)	$31,586 (25.8)
Large City or Village	15,310 (12.5)	2,785 (2.3)	18,095 (14.8)
Other	34,173 (28.0)	38,416 (31.4)	72,634 (59.4)
Total	65,805 (53.8)	56,510 (46.2)	122,315 (100.0)

* United States Bureau of the Census, *United States Census of Governments 1962*, Vol. VII, No. 32, Tables 32-34.

** The parenthesis figures indicate the percentage that the figure above it is of the total revenue, $122,315,000. A X^2 test for independence indicated that the joint probabilities are significanly different from the marginal probabilities at the .05 level, given two degrees of freedom. Thus the composition of revenues to the three types of governments is different.

cent of the revenues and over sixty per cent of the expenditures in 1962.

When the revenue data are restructured to indicate the differences in sources and levels of various revenues, the absolute dominance of Other governments in the Mohawk Region is again indicated: They received over one-half of local revenue and nearly three-fourths of inter-governmental revenue.

It is clear that "Large Cities and Villages" — those of population 10,000 and over in 1960 — received less than a proportionate share of intergovernmental revenue, *i.e.,* $(.462)(.148) = .068$ the proportionate share of inter-governmental revenue which is greater than .023 by .045. Or, given the level of Large City or Village revenue, \$8,317,000 should have been from inter-governmental revenue — to maintain proportionality — but actually \$2,785,000 came from inter-governmental revenue.

Table C-16 also indicates that inter-governmental revenue is quantitatively important — \$56,510,000 in 1962 and 46.2 per cent of all revenues — and it is also the fastest growing source of revenue for each type of government, as Table C-17 indicates.

Table C-17

Mohawk Region Local Government
Revenues Average Annual Growth Rates *
1962-1957

Region Governments	Revenues Own Sources (Per cent)	Inter-governmental Revenue (Per cent)	Total Revenue (Per cent)
County	7.9	11.1	9.4
Large City or Village	6.2	7.5	6.4
Other	6.4	9.4	7.9
Total	6.7	9.7	8.1

* United States Bureau of the Census, *United States Census of Governments 1962*, Vol. VII, No. 32, Tables 32, 33, and 34; *United States Census of Governments 1957*, Vol. V, No. 30, Tables 38 and 40.

In absolute figures, changes in revenues by source offer less possibility for generalization. Increases in large city or village revenues from inter-governmental sources were less than twenty per cent of their total revenue increase, while for the other two classes of governments, inter-governmental revenue provided more than fifty per cent of total revenue increases.

Comparing data presented in Table C-18 (percentage share of absolute increases) with the percentage share of total levels, indicates that there is an increasing shift of all revenue from large cities and villages; *i.e.,* 2.1 per cent of the increase in all revenues went to large cities and villages through inter-governmental revenue, but large cities and villages had 2.3 per cent of all revenues in 1962 in the same category. Since the marginal share — 1957-1962 — was below the average, the average has declined and the 1962 percentage share of revenues must have been below that for 1957.

Table C-18

Mohawk Region Local Government Changes in Revenues *
1962-1957

Region Governments	Revenue Own Sources (000)	Inter- governmental Revenue (000)	Total (000)
County	$5,180	$6,262	$11,442
	(13.2)**	(15.9)	(29.1)
Large City or Village	3,956	842	4,798
	(10.1)	(2.1)	(12.2)
Other	9,159	13,899	23,058
	(23.3)	(35.4)	(58.7)
Total	18,295	21,003	39,298
	(46.6)	(53.4)	(100.0)

* United States Bureau of the Census, *United States Census of Governments 1962,* Vol. VII, No. 32, Tables 32, 33, and 34; *United States Census of Governments 1957,* Vol. V, No. 30, Tables 38 and 40.

** The parenthesis data are the per cents the increases are of the total increase in revenue, $39,298,000.

Marginal and average rates may be subtracted to arrive at an indication of the trend in future fiscal receipts for the three types of governments. Positive numbers indicate a trend towards increasing importance relative to a total change in all revenues. These are not to be interpreted as declines in absolute levels — rather the correct generalization is that if the 1957 to 1962 trend continues, inter-governmental aid will be of increasing relative importance as a source of revenue and that county governments will be of increasing relative importance *vis-a-vis* large city and village governments and other governments. Thus the marginal percent share for county govern-ments' total revenue is 3.3 per cent above the same average per cent share and is the largest total revenue share. The trend is to-wards increasing revenue size of county governments relative to all public sector revenues received by Mohawk Region governments. This is due entirely to their marginal gain in inter-governmental revenue.

Table C-19

Mohawk Region Local Government 1962-1957 Marginal
Percent Shares of Revenues Minus 1962 Average
Percent Shares of Revenues*

Region Governments	Revenues Own Sources (Per cent)	Inter-governmental Revenues (Per cent)	Total Revenues (Per cent)
County	—.1	3.4	3.3
Large City or Village	—2.4	—.2	—2.6
Other	—4.7	4.0	—.7
Total	—7.2	7.2	0.0

* United States Bureau of the Census, *United States Census of Govern-ments 1962*, Vol. VII, No. 32, Tables 32, 33, and 34; *United States Census of Governments 1957*, Vol. V, No. 30, Tables 38 and 40.

Concerning expenditures made by the three types of governments in the Mohawk Region, comparative analysis yields some interesting conclusions. The expenditures are analyzed first by inputs or pur-chases — capital, labor, materials, and miscellaneous — and then by function of output — education, highways, health, hospitals, and welfare, etc. Again each is discussed in terms of level, share of change, and trend.

The data indicate the absolute importance of other governments in labor payroll, capital, and miscellaneous expenditures and that large cities and villages have the lowest level of expenditures. The composition of the expenditures in terms of inputs by types of government are also of interest. These percentages are listed below and indicate a large divergence in allocation to inputs for functional ex-

Table C-20

Mohawk Region Local Government Expenditure Levels by Characteristics of Inputs *
1962

Region Governments	Labor Payroll (000)	Capital (000)	Miscellaneous (000)	Total (000)
County	(7.3)**	(3.1)	(15.1)	(25.5)
	$9,000	$3,862	$18,707	$31,569
	(13.4)	(27.1)	(44.6)	
Large City or Village	(7.6)	(2.3)	(4.2)	(14.1)
	9,372	2,827	5,153	17,352
	(13.9)	(19.8)	(12.3)	
Other	(39.7)	(6.1)	(14.6)	(60.4)
	48,996	7,573	18,056	74,625
	(72.7)	(53.1)	(43.1)	
Total	(54.6)	(11.5)	(33.9)	(100.0)
	67,368	14,262	41,916	123,546
	(100.0)	(100.0)	(100.0)	(100.0)

* United States Bureau of the Census, *United States Census of Governments, 1962*, Vol. VII, No. 32, Tables 29-34.
** The percentage figures are included within the parenthesis. Those using the column totals as the base are included in the parenthesis below the whole numbers; the percentages using $123,546,000 as the base are included within the parenthesis above the whole numbers.

penditures by the local governments. The counties, being the main distributors of welfare expenditures and thus transfer payments, have a large allocation to the miscellaneous category of inputs. Subtracting from these, the per cent distribution between labor and capital indicates that county governments had a greater allocation to capital inputs than large cities or villages and other governments. Thus, of the $81,630,000 spent on capital and labor payroll in the Mohawk Region in 1962, $14,262,000 or 17.5 per cent of this went to capital or social overhead capital. Though over fifty-three per cent of this was spent by other governments, county governments in terms of per cent composition between capital and labor, had the greatest relative inputs of capital while other governments had the greatest relative

Table C-21

Percentage Composition of Expenditure Inputs by
Mohawk Region Governments *
1962

Region Governments	Labor Payroll (Per cent)	Capital (Per cent)	Miscellaneous (Per cent)	Total (Per cent)
Counties	28.5	12.2	59.3	100.0
Large Cities or Villages	54.0	16.3	29.7	100.0
Other Governments	65.7	10.1	24.2	100.0
Total	54.6	11.5	33.9	100.0

* United States Bureau of the Census, *United States Census of Governments 1962*, Vol. VII, No. 32, Tables 29-34.

input of labor payroll. Again, this is probably more a result of the governments' functional expenditure responsibilities than their relative efficiencies.

Table C-23 indicates the change in shares of labor payroll, capital, and miscellaneous expenditures in the Mohawk Region by type of government, 1957-1962. The table indicates that capital expenditures decreased by $3,300,000 between 1957 and 1962 and that county governments alone increased their capital outlays. Counties also exhibited the greatest growth in miscellaneous expenditures.

Table C-22

Composition of Capital and Labor Payroll Inputs in
Local Government Expenditures in the Mohawk Region *
1962

Region Governments	Percent Labor Payroll	Percent Capital	Total (000)
County	70.0	30.0	$12,862
Large Cities or Villages	76.8	23.2	12,199
Other Governments	86.6	13.4	56,569
Total	82.5	17.5	81,630

* United States Bureau of the Census, *United States Census of Governments 1962*, Vol. VII, No. 32, Tables 29-34.

Large cities and villages exhibited little growth in expenditures while other governments had the largest increase in total expenditures.

Using the functional expenditure categories of education, highways, health-hospital-welfare, police-fire, and residual for each of the three

Table C-23

Mohawk Region Local Government Changes in Expenditure for Inputs *
1962-1957

Region Governments	Labor Payroll (000)	Capital (000)	Miscellaneous (000)	Total (000)
County	$2,851	$443	$7,079	$10,373
Large City or Village	2,068	—1,040	—961	66
Other Governments	19,612	—2,742	2,211	19,081
Total	24,530	—3,339	8,329	29,520

* United States Bureau of the Census, *United States Census of Governments 1962*, Vol. VII, No. 32, Tables 29-34; *United States Census of Governments 1957*, Vol. VI, No. 30, Tables 23, 27, 36, and 37.

Table C-24

Mohawk Region Government Allocation of Change in Expenditure *
1962-1957

Region Governments	Education (000)	Highways (000)	Hospitals Health Welfare (000)	Police Fire (000)	Residual (000)	Total (000)
County	$1,347	$1,222	$7,152	$166	$486	$10,373
	(4.6)**	(4.1)	(24.2)	(.6)	(1.6)	(35.1)
Large City or Village	....	—697	345	920	—502	66
		(—2.4)	(1.2)	(3.1)	(—1.7)	(.2)
Other	17,179	397	797	550	158	19,081
	(58.2)	(1.3)	(2.7)	(1.9)	(.5)	(64.6)
Total	18,526	922	8,294	1,636	142	29,520
	(62.8)	(3.1)	(28.1)	(5.5)	(.5)	(100.0)

* United States Bureau of the Census, *United States Census of Governments 1962*, Vol. VII, No. 32, Tables 28 and 33; *United States Census of Governments 1957*, Vol. VI, No. 30, Tables 36 and 40.

** Percentage figures of the $29,520,000 base are included in parenthesis.

types of governments in the Mohawk Region, the changes in expenditures by functional categories were tabulated. These are indicated in the following table. The data indicate an increasing fiscal specialization by each type of local government in the Mohawk Region. Counties used nearly eighty-five per cent of their expenditure increase to provide health-hospital-welfare services. Their 1957 allocation to these categories was about fifty per cent. Large city or village governments used over thirteen times as much as their total expenditure increase to provide police-fire services. The excess came from absolute decreases in highway and residual expenditures. Other governments used ninety per cent of their expenditure increase to provide educational services with very small increases in the other functional services.

In summary, the trends and composition of changes in local fiscal policies can be listed:

1. The largest amount of local government expenditure by Mohawk Region local governments were made by other governments;

2. Inter-governmental revenues were quantitatively important and provided the largest increase in revenue though they were still less than one-half of all revenue received by large cities or villages and counties;

3. Other governments alone received more than one-half their total revenue from inter-governmental sources;

4. The largest marginal excess share of the increase in revenues were received by county governments;

5. The greatest amount of capital and labor payroll expenditures were made by other governments;

6. All capital expenditures were less than twelve per cent of all expenditures in 1962 and decreased by over three million dollars from 1957 with most of the marginal increase in expenditures for inputs going to labor payroll;

7. The change in expenditures by function and type of government indicates again the trend towards fiscal supremacy by county governments in health-hospitals-welfare expenditures and large city or village governments in police-fire services.

95

The Mohawk Region local government trend and functional composition of expenditures and the trend and composition of revenues are important for state planning. The local responsibilities for services and net effect of the myriad grant-in-aid formulas must be considered if the State is to take an active part in changing the level and composition of area services and the quality of the local environment.

Regional Income 1964

The simple statement that, total personal income[3] of the Mohawk Region was $1,106,600,000 for 1964, does not provide a meaningful indication of the level of personal income in the Mohawk Region: To present a deeper analysis, this discussion will center on four aspects of income: level, type, source, and distribution. For the most part, per capita incomes will be used for comparative purposes and, where appropriate, the income figures will be adjusted to 1963 price levels. The use of constant dollars provides a measure of real income by eliminating the effects on current dollar incomes of price level changes over time.[4] The level of adjusted per capita income in the Study Region is low, twelve per cent lower than that of the nation,

---

[3] Personal income is the income allocated to persons before deductions for income and other direct personal taxes but after deductions for personal contributions to social security and other social insurance programs, and includes both cash income and imputed income such as rent of owner-occupied dwellings.

[4] The adjustment for price changes was made by using the implicit price deflator for gross national product with 1963 = 100.0. This deflator series and base was used throughout the study whenever current money measures were transferred into constant purchasing values. Ideally, the deflator should be a regional price index series but such is not yet available. The use of the same price index series for all regions changes the current values by a constant and thus does not change the point inter-regional ratios though it does change the time-series values.

seven per cent lower than that of the upstate area, and thirty-six per cent lower than the State.[5]

Type of Income

A closer analysis of the Region's per capita income, and its disaggregation by type, indicates that the Region was lower than national standard in almost every category.[6] As can be seen, wage and salary and property incomes made up larger percentages of the Region's per capita income than they did of per capita income for the nation. Also, their concentration coefficients were higher than the Mohawk Region's concentration coefficient for total per capita income.

---

[5] The relation between per cent shares is similar to the relationship between concentration coefficients. If two per cent shares are different, then the two C.C.'s will be different. If the Mohawk share is lower *vis-a-vis* the United States, then the Mohawk concentration coefficient for that share will be lower than the Mohawk total C.C. If the Mohawk share is higher *vis-a-vis* the United States, then the Mohawk C.C. in that particular share will be higher than the total.

where:
Rm is the Mohawk Region
y is total personal income
p is population
w-s is wage and salary income
C.C. is concentration coefficient

$$(1) \quad \frac{Rm\ y/p}{U.S.\ y/p} = C.C._{Rm}^{y/p};$$

$$(2) \quad \frac{Rm\ w\text{-}s/p}{U.S.\ w\text{-}s/p} = C.C._{Rm}^{w\text{-}s};$$

$$(3) \quad \frac{Rm\ w\text{-}s/p}{Rm\ y/p} = w\text{-}s\ \frac{\%}{Rm}$$

$$(4) \quad Rm\ w\text{-}s/p = (C.C._{Rm}^{w\text{-}s})\ (U.S.w\text{-}s/p)$$

$$(5) \quad Rm\ y/p = \frac{Rm\ w\text{-}s/p}{w\text{-}s\ \dfrac{\%}{Rm}}$$

By substitution: (5 and 4)

$$(6) \quad Rm\ y/p = \frac{(C.C._{Rm}^{w\text{-}s})\ (U.S.\ w\text{-}s/p)}{(w\text{-}s\ \dfrac{\%}{Rm})}$$

By substitution:

$$(7) \quad C.C._{Rm}^{y/p} = \frac{(C.C._{Rm}^{w\text{-}s})\ (U.S.\ w\text{-}s/p)}{(w\text{-}s\ \dfrac{\%}{Rm})\ (U.S.\ y/p)} = (C.C._{Rm}^{w\text{-}s})\ (\frac{U.S.\ \dfrac{\%}{Rm}\ w\text{-}s)}{w\text{-}s\ \dfrac{\%}{}})$$

Therefore: if the ratio of the two percentages is equal to one then the two concentration coefficients are equal.

[6] Definitions for the types of income are: Salaries and Wages — Both private and government payments for services, including tips, commissions and payments in kind, but not employers' contributions to social insurance programs; Property — Rental income (and the imputed rent of owner-occupied homes), dividends, interest, and royalties; Proprietors'— The net business

97

In every category except one, the concentration coefficients for personal income by type show that the Mohawk Region was lower than the nation. The exception is in the classification "Other" which was seven per cent greater. This category consists primarily of net incomes derived from transfer payments, both private and public. Public or government transfers in the form of unemployment insurance, old age and survivors benefits, and workmen's compensation made up the bulk of this income.

As the "Total" column indicates, the twelve per cent lower wages and salaries income received in the Mohawk Region, compared to the nation, was not offset by the seven per cent higher "Other" income. If the Region had average United States per capita property,

Table C-25

Adjusted Per Capita Income by Type *
1964

	Total	Wages and Salaries	Property	Farm	Proprietors' Business and Profes- sional	Other
Nation	$2,518 ~~$2,518~~	$1,698	$355	$60	$199	$206
New York	3,103	2,076	543	12	230	242
Upstate	2,423	1,689	342	36	148	208
Region	2,208	1,499	329	43	117	220
	Per Cent Shares in Per Capita Income					
Nation	100.0	67.4	14.1	2.4	7.9	8.2
New York	100.0	66.9	17.5	.4	7.4	7.8
Upstate	100.0	69.7	14.1	1.5	6.1	8.6
Region	100.0	67.8	14.9	1.9	5.3	10.0
	Per Capita Income Concentration Coefficient					
Nation	1.000	1.000	1.000	1.000	1.000	1.000
New York	1.232	1.223	1.530	.200	1.156	1.175
Upstate	.962	.995	.963	.600	.743	1.010
Region	.877	.882	.927	.717	.588	1.068

* New York State Department of Commerce, *Personal Income in Counties of New York State 1964* (Albany, 1966), pp. 10-11; *Survey of Current Business,* July, 1965, p. 12.

earnings of owners of unincorporated enterprises, including farms; Other — Employer contributions to private pension plans and group insurance, compensation to individuals for injuries, old age and survivors benefits, unemployment insurance, relief, military pensions, and payments by the business system not in the form of earnings for participation in production — less the current contributions of employees and the self-employed to these programs.

farm, and business and professional incomes, its per capita income would have been $2,333, an increase of $125 or a total ninety-three per cent of the United States per capita. On the other hand, by raising the Region's wage and salary income levels to United States standard, adjusting other incomes downward, and leaving the three remaining classifications of income as they were, we would cause the regional per capita to increase by $185 to $2,393. This new per capita remains below the United States average, but it is two per cent above what would have resulted from changes of the first sort. The net gain in the first case was $125 per capita and in the second case it was $185 per capita; or, there would be a forty-eight per cent difference in the Region's total per capita income. The importance of wage and salary incomes as a percentage of total per capita income is highlighted by these estimates.

Source of Income

An additional disaggregation of per capita personal income which affords insight into the composition of regional incomes is income by source.[7]

Concentration coefficients and percentage shares of government, as a source of income, were higher in the Mohawk Region, while farm and private non-farm income were both lower. While farms were a more important source of income for the Region than for the other areas of New York State, they were not as important a source of income as they were for the nation as a whole. Government share in the Region was higher than for the two areas of the State drawn for comparative purposes, but all three New York State areas had greater than national percentages attributable to government. This may be due in part to New York's social welfare programs as compared to those of other states and localities and to New York's government employment and pay patterns.

The reasons for the low per capita income in the Region in each category of type and source, except for Other and Government, are

---

[7] Definitions of income by source are: Government — Income derived from governmental sources as wages, salaries, pensions, unemployment benefits and relief; Farm — Income derived by proprietors, tenants, and employees from operation of privately-owned farms; Private, Non-farm — All personal income other than Government and Farm.

Table C-26

Adjusted Per Capita Income by Source *
1964

	Total	Farm Incomes	Government Income Disbursements	Private Non-Farm Incomes
Nation	$2,518	$75	$500	$1,943
New York	3,103	19	541	2,543
Upstate	2,423	47	506	1,870
Region	2,208	52	610	1,546
Per Cent Shares in Per Capita Income				
Nation	100.0	3.0	19.8	77.2
New York	100.0	.6	17.4	82.0
Upstate	100.0	1.9	20.9	77.2
Region	100.0	2.4	2.7	70.0
Per Capita Income Concentration Coefficient				
Nation	1.000	1.000	1.000	1.000
New York	1.232	.253	1.082	1.309
Upstate	.962	.629	1.012	.962
Region	.877	.693	1.220	.796

* New York State Department of Commerce, *Personal Income in Counties of New York State 1964* (Albany, 1966), pp. 10-11; *Survey of Current Business*, July, 1965, p. 12.

not at all clear or easily discernible. The low per capita income may be due to: (1) lower than national average participation rates; (2) lower than average private wage and salaries, and receipts from wealth; and/or (3) less than continuous full employment, high levels of long-term unemployment, or widespread partial employment. These three areas will be discussed and analyzed more fully in later sections of this report, along with the factors of employment and industry.

Distribution of Income

The previous discussion of income centered on the questions of level, type, and source. The primary question remaining is how the income which had been earned from various sources was distributed among the Region's population. This portion of the study will be

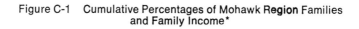

Figure C-1　Cumulative Percentages of Mohawk **Region** Families
and Family Income*

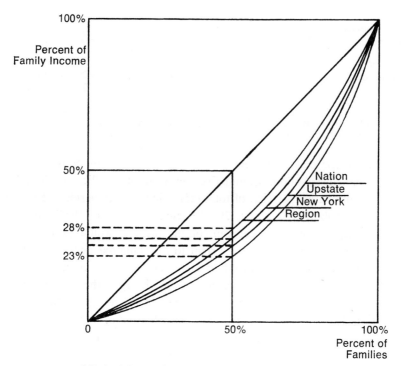

* United States Bureau of the Census, *United States Census
of Population 1960,* Vol. I, Pt. 1, Table 95; Pt. 34, Tables 66 and 86.

concerned primarily with distribution of family incomes, with some discussion of income shares by sex and by race.

Table C-27

Distribution of Family Income *
1959

Per Cent of Incomes:	Per Cent of Families						
	0	10	25	50	75	90	100
Nation	0	1	7	23	49	71	100
New York	0	2	8	26	53	75	100
Upstate	0	2	8	25	51	72	100
Region	0	2	9	28	54	76	100

* United States Bureau of the Census, *United States Census of Population 1960*, Vol. I, Pt. 34, Tables 66 and 86; Pt. I, Table 95.

The Lorenz curve has become a standard method of presentation of income distribution. Cumulative per cent of families is plotted against cumulative per cent of total family income. A perfectly equal income distribution; *i.e.*, 10, 20, 30, etc., per cent of the families having 10, 20, 30, etc., per cent of the income, would produce a forty-five degree line from the origin to one hundred per cent. The closer the curve is to the forty-five degree line, the greater the degree of income equality; the further it is from the line, the greater the inequality. On this basis, it can be seen from the graph that the Mohawk Region had a more equal distribution of family income than either New York State or the upstate area, though both of these

Table C-28

Concentration Coefficient of Family Incomes *
1959

	$0-$3,000	$3,000-$10,000	$10,000 and Over
Nation	1.000	1.000	1.000
New York	.645	1.044	1.318
Upstate	.696	1.109	1.040
Region	.692	1.134	.874

* United States Bureau of the Census, *United States Census of Population 1960*, Vol. I, Pt. 34, Tables 66 and 86; Pt. I, Table 95.

areas, as well as the Region, had more equal distributions than that for the nation as a whole. The distributions of family incomes in 1959 follows.[8] The 1959 data are the most current. The table and the curve show that for each category of per cent of families, families in the Region have a larger percentage of total family income than families in the nation. For example, the first twenty-five per cent of the Mohawk Region's families have nine per cent of the income, while for the nation the first twenty-five per cent have seven per cent of the income, and the same pattern exists to one hundred per cent.

Concentration coefficients of family incomes for 1959 display the same relationship as indicated by the Lorenz curve; *i.e.,* a smaller per cent of families in the $0 to $3,000 and $10,000 and over categories, but a larger per cent in the $3,000 to $10,000 category than the national average.

Table C-29

Total Income of Individuals *
1959

	Total	Male	Female
Nation (000,000)	$344,556.8	$275,103.0	$69,453.8
Per cent	100.0	79.8	20.2
New York (000,000)	37,530.2	29,268.7	82,615.0
Per cent	100.0	78.0	22.0
Upstate (000,000)	11,621.9	8,974.1	2,647.8
Per cent	100.0	77.2	22.8
Region (000,000)	833.9	673.9	160.0
Per cent	100.0	80.8	19.2

* United States Bureau of the Census, *United States Census of Population 1960,* Vol. I, Pt. 34, Tables 66 and 86; Pt. I, Table 95.

[8] The income figures are derived from the *United States Census of Population* and differ from the personal income estimates previously used, mostly by ignoring non-cash income. The estimate of Mohawk total income derived from the *Census* was about $100 million less than that estimated by the New York Department of Commerce.

The availability of data in the 1960 *Census of Population* permits disaggregation of incomes to individuals by sex.[9]

Table C-30

Income-Receiving Population, Percent Male-Female*
1959

	Total	Male	Female
Nation	$90,454,556	$55,164,237	$35,290,319
Per cent	100.0	61.0	39.0
New York	8,882,878	5,280,534	3,602,344
Per cent	100.0	59.4	40.6
Upstate	3,130,597	1,878,356	1,252,241
Per cent	100.0	60.0	40.0
Region	223,688	124,449	99,234
Per cent	100.0	55.6	44.4

* United States Bureau of the Census, *United States Census of Population 1960*, Vol. I, Pt. 34, Tables 66 and 86; Pt. I, Table 95.

Table C-31

Per Capita Individual Income *
1959

	Total	Male	Female
Nation	$3,809	$4,986	$1,968
New York	4,225	5,543	2,293
Upstate	3,712	4,778	2,114
Region	3,727	5,415	1,612

* United States Bureau of the Census, *United States Census of Population 1960*, Vol. I, Pt. 34, Tables 66 and 86; Pt. I, Table 95.

As indicated by the tables, female income receivers in the Region obtained a smaller share of total income but constituted a higher percentage of income receivers than did females in the other three areas. Therefore, women in the Region received less income per capita— $1,612 — and the Region had more women receiving less income, on the average, than did the United States.

---

[9] Income data are in current dollars.

Discussions of income often rely heavily on the use of median family income statistics as a basis of inter-regional comparisions. The median figure is the half-way figure of the distribution, half the population displaying the characteristic being measured lying above the median point and half lying below. To say an area has a median family income of $2,000 per year means that half the families having income earn more than $2,000 per year and half earn less. Median family income in the Region is considerably lower than the national or state standard.

Table C-32

Median Family Income *
1959

	Median Income
Nation	$5,660
New York	6,371
Upstate	6,072
Region	5,184

* United States Bureau of the Census, *United States Census of Population 1960*, Vol. I, Pt. 34, Tables 66 and 86; Pt. I, Table 95.

Although data concerning incomes of non-white populations are not available for the entire Region, some information is available for Oneida County, which contains the bulk — eighty-eight per cent — of the Region's non-white persons. Median family income for the 987 non-white families in Oneida County was $3,687 in 1959, compared to $6,180 for all Oneida families. This last figure would, of course, have been higher if incomes of white families only had been recorded. Forty per cent of all families in Oneida County with incomes of $3,000 or less were non-white. Out of the 987 non-white families in that county, 398 were below the $3,000 poverty level while fourteen per cent of all Oneida families had incomes below that level.

Regional Income: 1948-1964

During the period of 1948 to 1964, total personal income of the Mohawk Region, in current dollars, grew from $578.2 million to $1,107.6 million, a rate of 4.1 per cent. This growth rate, however, was lower than those for either the United States, New York State, or upstate, each of which more than doubled their total personal income. As stated earlier, a better picture of income growth is gained when incomes are adjusted over time for price level changes and are presented in constant dollar terms. When such an adjustment is made for income growth during the sixteen-year period, the results are as shown in the following table. The base year is 1963.

Growth rate of adjusted total personal income for the 1948-1964 period for the Region was 2.1 per cent, again lower than either the United States, New York, or upstate.

Deviations of growth rates around the mean growth rates are presented in Table C-33. Deviations are measured by the coefficient of variation (C.V.)[10] The C.V. is higher for the Mohawk Region than for the three comparison areas during the 1948-1964 period, indicating that rates of total income growth in the Region had a larger amount of variation around the 1948-1964 trend than did those of the United States and New York. On this basis, the "average" growth rate for the 1948-1964 period in the Mohawk Region is not a perfectly "reliable" description of the rate of income growth.

Combining changes in the rate of population growth with changes in the rate of total personal income, to arrive at growth rates in per capita personal income, provides a fuller picture of change in economic welfare within the Region. Using constant rather than current dollar income provides a better measure of change in the real per capita income.

---

[10] The formula for standard deviation and coefficient of variation are as follows:

$$\text{standard deviation} = \sqrt{\frac{(\bar{x}-x)^2}{n-1}}$$

$$\text{cofficient of variation} = \frac{\text{standard deviation}}{\bar{x}} \times 100$$

where: $\bar{x}$ is the mean

x is the value of an individual item

n is the number of items

The coefficient of variation is smaller if unadjusted total personal income is used.

Table C-33

Growth Rates of Adjusted Personal Income *
1964-1948

	Total Personal Income 1964 (000,000)	Growth Rate Total Personal Income (Per cent)	Mean Rate (Per cent)	Standard Deviation (Per cent)	Coefficient of Variation (Per cent)
Nation	$481,848.9	3.5	3.4	1.173	34.2
New York	55,592.7	3.0	3.0	1.188	40.1
Upstate	15,863.3	2.8	2.8	1.289	45.8
Region	1,086.9	2.1	2.2	1.013	47.1

* New York State Department of Commerce, *Personal Income in Counties of New York State 1963* (Albany, 1965), p. 14; *Personal Income in Counties in New York State 1964* (Albany, 1966), p. 10; *Survey of Current Business,* April, 1966, p. 11.

Table C-34

Adjusted Per Capita Personal Income *
1964-1948

	Per Capita Income 1948	Per Capita Income 1964	Growth Rate (Per cent)	Mean Growth Rate (Per cent)	Standard Deviation (Per cent)	Coefficient of Variation (Per cent)
Nation	$1,901	$2,518	1.8	2.1	1.230	59.3
New York	2,407	3,103	1.6	1.6	1.138	70.6
Upstate	1,997	2,423	1.2	1.2	1.354	110.5
Region	1,896	2,207	1.0	1.0	.964	101.4

* New York State Department of Commerce, *Personal Income in Counties of New York State 1963* (Albany, 1965), p. 14; *Personal Income in Counties in New York State 1964* (Albany, 1966), p. 10; *Survey of Current Business,* April, 1966, p. 11.

The rate of growth of per capita personal income in the Mohawk Region was lower than the rate experienced by the other areas used for comparison. Although the levels of per capita income for the nation and the Region were quite close in 1948, the differences in the rates of growth have caused these levels to diverge considerably during the sixteen-year period. Again, as with the rates of growth of total personal income, the Mohawk Region has a larger C.V. than that of the nation, indicating a larger variation in growth rates for the Region than for the United States.

107

Type of Income

Continuing the examination of changes in personal income between 1948 and 1964, attention will be given to the developments which took place in the composition of income by type.

Inspection of Table C-35 indicates a considerable variation in changes of income by type. For the nation, wages and salaries, property, and other incomes increased more than did total personal income, while business and professional income increased somewhat less and farm income was negative — actually lost income. New York State, upstate, and the Region experienced less than the national increases in each income category except in the area of farm income, where they had less of a decrease than the nation.

Table C-35

Percent Changes in Total Personal Income by Type
(Unadjusted) *
1964-1948

	Total Personal Income	Wages and Salaries	Property	Farm	Business and Professional	Other
Nation	135.2	146.7	199.8	—32.5	74.5	244.4
New York	117.4	112.9	169.0	—27.4	63.7	164.4
Upstate	111.7	115.2	135.1	—24.9	65.0	170.4
Region	91.6	89.6	135.6	—15.0	43.7	143.4

* New York State Department of Commerce, *Personal Income in Counties of New York State 1963* (Albany, 1965), p. 14; *Personal Income in Counties of New York State 1964* (Albany, 1966), p. 10; United States Department of Commerce, *Statistical Abstract of the United States 1966*, p. 328.

A question which may be asked is, "How much would incomes have increased had they increased at a standard rate?" Several different standards could be used: the per cent increase in the nation's total personal income; separate rates of changes for different types of incomes; or New York State or upstate per cent changes in total or types of incomes.

Applying national average per cent changes for total income and types of income to the 1948 base for the Mohawk Region produces the following 1964 results.

Table C-36

Mohawk Region Personal Income, Actual and
Standard Changes, (in millions of dollars) *
1964-1948

Mohawk Region Income	Wages and Total Salaries		Property	Farm	Business and Professional	Other
(1) Actual, 1964	$1,107.6	$752.1	$164.9	$21.6	$58.5	$110.5
(2) Expected, 1964	1,433.1	978.7	209.9	17.1	71.0	156.4
(3) Actual Change (1964-1948)	529.4	355.4	94.9	—3.8	17.8	65.1
(4) Expected Change (1964-1948)	854.9	582.0	139.9	—8.3	30.3	111.0
(5) Per Cent Difference (4 — 3 ÷ 4)	(38.1)	(38.9)	(32.2)	(54.2)	(41.2)	(41.3)

* New York State Department of Commerce, *Personal Income in Counties of New York State 1963* (Albany, 1965), p. 14; *Personal Income in Counties of New York State 1964* (Albany, 1966), p. 10; United States Department of Commerce, *Statistical Abstract of the United States 1966*, p. 328.

If each type of regional personal income had grown at the national rate between 1948 and 1964, the Mohawk Region would have had a total personal income of $1,433.1 million rather than its actual income of $1,107.6 million, nearly one-third of a billion more. The picture might be dramatized more clearly by comparing only the actual and standard changes rather than the totals for the 1948-1964 period. In each case, except farm, the discrepancy of actual regional income change from the standard change was less than fifty per cent. Quantitatively, the most important deviation from the national standard for the 1948-1964 period is wages and salaries. Its absolute deficiency from the standard amount was $226.6 million which is 69.6 per cent of the total deficit recorded by the Region.

Changes in income relationships by type for the sixteen-year-period, 1948-1964, are presented on the following graphs. The Region displays a growth in property incomes and other incomes, each as a per cent of wages and salaries, greater than those for the nation. Business and professional and farm incomes, as per cents of wage and salary income, registered declines during this time period. Between 1948 and 1964, property incomes and other incomes grew as a percentage of total personal income, while other types of income declined as a percentage.

Graph C-1   Changes in type of income*

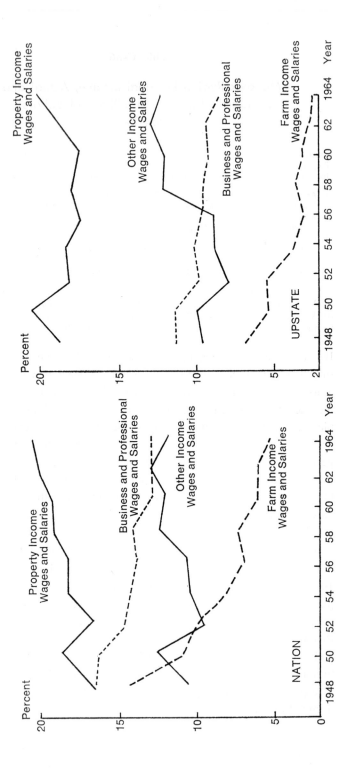

Changes in Type of Income (cont.) *
Graph C-1

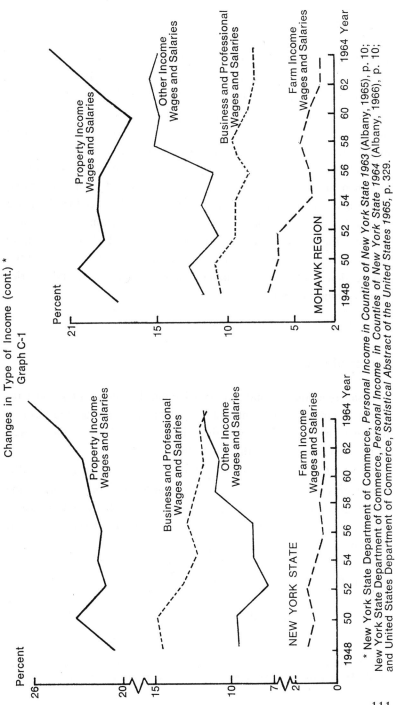

* New York State Department of Commerce, *Personal Income in Counties of New York State 1963* (Albany, 1965), p. 10;
New York State Department of Commerce, *Personal Income in Counties of New York State 1964* (Albany, 1966), p. 10;
and United States Department of Commerce, *Statistical Abstract of the United States 1965*, p. 329.

111

A suggested explanation of why wages and salaries in the Region differ so greatly from what might have been expected on the basis of United States growth—a difference of $226.6 million—is the income effect of net regional commuting. If the figures used in the computation had been income earned in the region rather than income received in the Region, would the Region's wages and salaries income have been much closer to the national average? Based on information available, the answer is negative. In the sixteen-year period, wages and salaries earned in the Mohawk Region was thirty million dollars less than the growth in wages and salaries received. This means that if one had used wages and salaries where earned rather than by place of residence to account for the commuters' portion of wages and salaries, the income received in the Mohawk Region would have deviated further from the national average. Between 1948 and 1964, the Region gained thirty million dollars net in wages and salaries from commuting out.

Source of Income

Disaggregation of total personal income by source of income receipts — farm, government disbursements, and private non-farm — indicates the degree to which these have changed in amount as well as in composition during the 1950-1964 period.[11]

Graphs C-2 and C-3, plotting farm income and government disbursements as percentages of private non-farm income, indicate the major trends in income by source for the Mohawk Region. Government as a source of income was, by far, the largest relative gainer. It grew from 21.7 per cent of private non-farm income in the Mohawk Region to 39.5 per cent, a considerably greater percentage growth than in the nation. Farm income as a per cent of private non-farm income declined less rapidly for the region than for the nation, but at a rate similar to that for Upstate New York.

---

[11] Income by source has been calculated for the 1948-1964 period where available, and for the 1950-1964 period for the remainder of the data.

Graph C-2   Farm Income as a percent or private non-farm income
1948-1964 *

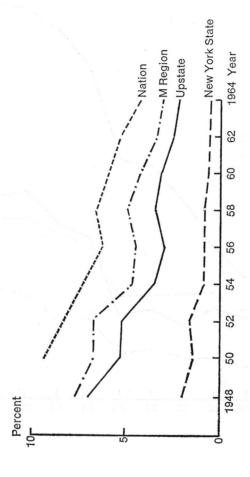

* New York State Department of Commerce, *Personal Income in Counties of New York State 1963* (Albany, 1965), p. 10;
New York State Department of Commerce, *Personal Income in Counties of New York State 1964* (Albany, 1966), p. 10;
and *Survey of Current Business,* July, 1960, p. 10 and July, 1965, p. 12.

Graph C-3 Government Income Disbursements as a percent of private
non-farm income 1948-1964 *

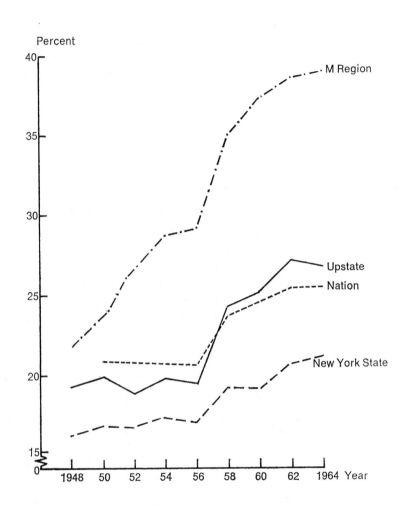

* New York State Department of Commerce, *Personal Income in Counties
of New York State 1963* (Albany, 1965), p. 10; New York State Department of
Commerce,*Personal Income in Counties of New York State1964*(Albany,1966),
p. 10; and *Survey of Current Business,* July, 1960, p. 10 and July, 1965, p. 12.

114

Regional Income Differentials

Total and per capita incomes of persons in the Mohawk Region differ substantially from what one could expect had the Region experienced growth rates similar to those of the nation. The following analyses have been developed in an attempt to better understand the causes of regional income differentials, and to provide a possible base for future action.

On the basis of population and per capita income, the Mohawk Region had a total income differential of $58.8 million. This is established by estimating what the total personal income would have been if regional per capita incomes had equaled the United States average, and then comparing this figure with the actual total income of the Region. A further step in disaggregating the existing income differential is to divide total income into property and non-property income. Non-property income is analogous to participation income, a commonly used concept. When this breakdown is made, it is apparent that non-property income accounts for $33.1 million of the total deficit, and property income for $25.7 million.

The complete analysis of income differentials based on population is presented as follows (M = Mohawk Region).

(1) M Population, 1960   =   466,831 persons

(2) M Total Personal Income, 1960   = $ 954.2 million

(3) M Per Capita Personal Income
(TPI), 1960   = $2,044.0

(4) U.S. Per Capita Personal Income,
1960   = $2,170.0

(5) M Standard TPI, 1960 = (1) x (4)   = $1,013.0 million

(6) M Differential Per Capita Income,
1960 = (4 - 3)   = $ 126.0

(7) M Differential TPI, 1960 - (5 - 2)   = $ 58.8 million

Disaggregating total income differential by type of income provides the following results.

115

(8) Actual TPI by Type, 1960
    (a) Property Income   = $ 109.7 million
    (b) Non-Property Income   = $ 844.5 million

(9) U.S. TPI (percent shares), 1960
    (a) Property Income   =   13.36 percent
    (b) Non-Property Income   =   86.64 percent

(10) M TPI by Type at Standard Totals, 1960
    (a) Property Income = ($1013.0)
    (13.36%)   = $ 135.4 million
    (b) Non-Property Income =
    ($1013.0)(86.64%)   = $ 877.6 million

(11) Differentials in TPI by Type
    (a) Property Income =
      (10a) - (8a)   = $ 25.7 million
    (b) Non-Property Income =
      (10b) - (8b)   = $ 33.1 million

                 Total Differential for M. $ 58.8 million

It is possible to establish the total income differential of the Mohawk Region based on labor force participation rather than on population. This type of analysis provides an estimate of the income differential traceable to participation or non-property income. The total differential established by this method — $64.4 million — is higher than that estimated for non-property income on a population basis — $33.1 million. This difference is a result of changing the base from total population to labor force.

(1) M Participation in Labor Force
    (L.F.), 1960   =   186,972 persons

(2) M Non-Property Income, 1960   = $ 844.5 million

(3) M Non-Property Income per L.F.
    member, 1960 = (2) ÷ (1)   = $4,517.0

(4) M Participation Rate as Percent of
    Persons 14 years +   =   55.9%

(5) U.S. Participation Rate as Percent of
    Persons 14 years +   =   55.3%

116

(6) M Expected L.F. = (M Pop. 14 years
+) x (55.3%)   =   185,113 persons

(7) U.S. Non-Property Income per L.F.
Member, 1960   = $4,861.0

(8) M Actual Non-Property Income, 1960
= (1) x (3)   = $ 844.5 million

    Less M Expected Non-Property In-
    come at U.S. Non-Property In-
    come per L.F. Member = (1) x
    (7)   = $ 908.9 million

    Deficit   = $ 64.4 million

The Mohawk Region actually had a labor force participation rate higher than that of the nation — 55.9 per cent compared to 55.3 per cent — and so had 1,859 more persons in the labor force than could have been expected given the national average. The extra participants provided an additional amount of income to the Mohawk Region's total, and so, the Region's total deficit in income was less than it might have been had it experienced the national rate of participation. This difference is shown by the analysis below.

(1) M, Actual Non-Property Income in
1960 = (1) x (3)   = $ 844.5 million

    Less M Expected Non-Property In-
    come with National Participation
    Rate and M Non-Property Income
    per L.F. Member, 1960 = (6) x
    (3)   = $ 836.2 million

(2) M gain from added Participation   =   8.3 million

The differential in total personal income of the Mohawk Region, based on labor force participation in 1960, totaled $64.4 million. This figure would have been $8.3 million higher, or $72.7 million, had the Region not had an additional 1,859 persons in its labor force. This deficit, $64.4 million after the participation adjustment, must be explained as a result of factors other than labor force participation in the Region, and this will be attempted below.

Income Differentials and Unemployment. The previous discussion of the income differentials of the Mohawk Region — the difference between the level of actual income and the level which could be expected using the nation as a standard — has established the amount of the differential which is attributable to deficient property income receipts and excess labor force participation. The amount of the gap in total income attributable to the difference in unemployment rates can now be included in the analysis.

(1) M standard non-property income
      = (a) (b)   == $ 950.8 million
    (a) U.S. employment rate of .944
        times
        M actual labor force 186,972
        = 176,502
    (b) U.S. non-property income of
        $348.2 billion divided by U.S.
        employment of 64,639,247 ==
        $5,386.8

(2) M actual non-property income   == $ 844.5 million
    Differential due to low receipts and
    excess unemployment and excess
    participation   == $ 106.3 million

(3) Income lost through excess unemploy-
        ment = $29.2 + $2.6 million   == $ 31.8 million
    (a) M standard employment of
        176,502 minus M actual
        employment of 170,602
    (b) M actual non-property income
        per employee of $4,950
    (c) U.S. non-property income per
        U.S. employee minus M non-
        property income per employee
        of $437

(4) Remaining differential due to low
      receipts per employee including
      excess participation
      ($106.3 – $29.2)   == $ 77.1 million

The above analysis indicates that the Mohawk Region, in 1959, had a total non-property income of $844.5 million compared to an expected standard non-property income of $950.8 million. The Region realized only 88.8 per cent of its expected standard, leaving $106.3 million, or 11.2 per cent, to be analyzed and explained. It has been shown that excess unemployment accounted for a loss in non-property income of $29.2 million or 3.1 per cent of the income differential. The remaining 8.1 per cent will be examined in the discussions of the structure of occupation and industry of the Region since the major factors to be considered in explaining the income gap are differential wage rates by occupation and the mix of high and low wage industries established in the Mohawk Region.

Wage and Salary Differentials. Having previously established for the Region an increasingly favorable — in terms of employment growth — occupational mix for males and an increasingly unfavorable mix for females, the question arises whether the mix also is favorable and unfavorable for increases in wages and salaries. There are two possible explanations for the previously determined income differential which involves the occupational mix: there may be a mix of low-paying occupations; or, the mix of occupations may be favorable for high wages and salaries but pay lower wages and salaries relative to the nation. These two possibilities will be examined.

The hypothesis regarding wage and salary income for the Mohawk Region which is to be tested is as follows: The Region has below national average wage and salary receipts per employee because the Region has a predominance of occupations which in the nation pay less than the national all-employment median income.

The method devised to test this hypothesis requires first that United States percentage shares of employment by occupation be applied to the Mohawk Region's occupational base to provide an estimate of expected mix of occupations for the Region, and, secondly, the actual Regional employment mix be compared to the expected mix. The median national wage and salary rate for each of the occupation categories is multiplied by these differences and the totals are summed.[12]

---

[12] Median wage and salary values are used here rather than mean values because of data availability. It is cautioned that such use of medians rather than means will produce results which are not fully comparable, unless the distributions being discussed are close to normal.

Based on national median wages and salaries, both male and female employment in the Region had a "favorable" or high wage

Table C-37

Analysis of Distribution of Employment by Occupation*
1960

	Total	PTK	FFM	M	CLS	CFK	OK	SPH	FL	OL	NR
Mohawk Per Cent Distribution											
Males	100.0	11.0	4.8	9.3	13.4	19.3	23.2	6.6	2.5	5.5	4.5
Females	100.0	13.7	.5	3.2	33.8	1.3	24.2	16.6	1.8		5.1
United States Per Cent Distribution											
Males	100.0	10.3	5.5	10.6	13.8	19.5	19.9	6.1	2.8	6.9	4.6
Females	100.0	13.0	.6	3.7	37.6	1.2	15.4	21.3	1.7		5.6
(1) Expected Mohawk, (000) Males											
	111.0	11.4	6.1	11.8	15.3	21.6	22.1	6.8	3.1	7.7	5.1
(2) Actual Mohawk, (000) Males											
	111.0	12.2	5.3	10.3	14.9	21.4	25.7	7.3	2.8	6.2	4.9
(3) Differences (000)											
	±4.9	+.8	−.8	−1.5	−.4	−.2	+3.6	+5.0	−.3	−1.5	−.2
(4) U.S. Median, Wage and Salary											
	$6,619	2,169	6,664	4,884	5,240	4,299	3,260	1,066	2,948	4,114	
(3) x (4), (000,000)											
	−$20.2 +22.4	+5.3	−1.7	−10.0	−2.0	−1.0	+15.5	+1.6	−.3	−4.4	−.8

+$2.2 million differential attributed to occupational mix of males.

	Total	PTK	FFM	M	CLS	CFK	OK	SPH	FL	OL	NR
(1) Expected Mohawk, (000) Females											
	59.7	7.8	.4	2.2	22.4	.7	9.2	12.7	1.0		3.3
(2) Actual Mohawk, (000) Females											
	59.7	8.2	.3	1.9	20.1	.8	14.4	9.9	1.1		3.0
(3) Differences (000)											
	±5.8	+4.0	−.1	−.3	−2.3	+.1	+5.2	−.3	+.1		−.3
(4) U.S. Median, Wage and Salary											
	$2,257	3,625	836	3,355	2,714	2,927	2,319	1,128	1,172		2,187
(3) x (4), (000,000)											
	−$11.2 +14.0 Total	+1.5	−.1	−1.0	−6.2	+.3	+12.1	−3.2	+.1		−.7

+$2.8 million differential attributed to occupational mix of females.

* United States Bureau of the Census, *United States Census of Population 1960*, Vol. I, Pt. 34, Table 84; Pt. 1, Tables 87 and 98. The column abbreviations indicate respectively: Professional, Technical and Kindred (PTK), Farm and Farm Managers (FFM), Other Managers (M), Clerical and Sales (CLS), Craftsmen, Foreman and Kindred (CFM), Operatives and Kindred (OK), Service and Private Household (SPH), Farm Labor (FL), Other Labor (OL), Labor (L), Not Reported (NR).

occupational mix in 1960 — $2.8 and $2.2 million. The hypothesis postulated above is therefore not acceptable given the data. The previously established gap in regional total non-property income of $106.3 million (less than $29.2 million due to excess unemployment) cannot be explained on the basis of an unfavorable mix of employment by occupation.

Accepting a favorable occupation mix for males and females for the Region compared to the nation, one should find as a complementary result that the median incomes of either or both males and females in the Mohawk Region are higher than the nation's median incomes.

Table C-38

Median Wage Rate*
1959

	Male	Female
Nation	$4,621	$2,257
New York	5,019	2,716
Region	4,495	2,866

* United States Bureau of the Census, *United States Census of Population 1960*, Vol. I, Pt. 34, Tables 67 and 86; Pt. 1, Table 98.

In fact, only the median wage rate for males is below the national median. The median wage rate for females is, as it should be above the national median. Thus only the males employed in the Mohawk Region receive less than in the nation for the same occupations, and their low wages and salaries *must be* a major cause of low per employee receipts in the Region.

Industrial Source of Income Differentials. This discussion will follow, in general form, the following order: an examination of the change in the level of income for the Mohawk Region, an analysis of the composition of the regional income, and an analysis of the change in income receipts per worker in the Region.

Total wages and salaries are 69.8 per cent of the Region's total personal income, and the data used apply to wage and salary disbursements of firms in the Region only, which is seven million dollars less than total wages and salaries received by residents of the

Table C-39

Per Cent Distribution of Employment and Wages and Salaries *
1960

	Census Employment Data (Mohawk 1960) (Per cent)	Establishment Wages and Salaries Data (Mohawk 1960) (Per cent)
Total	100.0	100.0
AFF	5.7	.9
C & M	4.8	3.7
Mfg.	36.5	40.7**
T P U C	4.8	5.7**
W R T	15.1	14.0
F I R E	3.1	3.0
SPA	26.3	31.5**
NR	3.7	—

* United States Bureau of the Census, *United States Census of Population 1960*, Vol. I, Pt. 34, Table 85; New York State Department of Commerce, *Personal Income in Counties of New York State 1960* (Albany, 1962), pp. 10-11.

** Indicates per cent of wages and salaries is above per cent employment for the industry.

Region. This seven million dollar difference is due to the net excess wage and salary income earned by residents who are the net commuters from the Region to other areas for employment. The net gain in wages and salary income in the Mohawk Region from out-commuting has increased since 1948. Without deducting the wages earned by net in-commuters, $404.7 million was paid out by firms within the Region and $396.7 million was received by residents of the Region in 1948. By 1964, $720.1 million was paid out within the Region and $730.1 million was received by regional residents. During this sixteen-year period, 1948-1964, the balance of commuting had shifted in the Mohawk Region from a net in-flow of commuters to a net out-flow.

Growth rates for wage and salary incomes by source were generally lower for the Mohawk Region than for the nation, but the Region did attain higher rates of wage-salary growth than did the nation in service-public administration, and wholesale-retail trade. The Region

Table C-40

Wages and Salaries by Source *
1964-1948

	Nation	New York	Upstate	Region
	1964 Total (millions)			
	$332,150.0	$39,164.0	$11,221.0	$741.0
	1948-1964 Change (millions)			
	$198,358.0	$20,778.0	$5,994.0	$336.3
	Growth Rates 1948-1964 (Per cent)			
Total	5.9	4.8	4.9	3.9
AFF	— 0.6	— 2.0	— 2.0	— 2.7
C&M	6.5	6.0	6.6**	5.4
Mfg.	5.2	3.7	3.7	1.3
TPUC	4.2	3.8	3.2	3.6
WRT	2.0	4.3**	5.6**	5.2**
FIRE	7.5	5.9	7.1	6.2
SPA	. 7.8	7.0	6.9	8.0**
Other	1.6	4.5**	3.5**	4.9**

* *Survey of Current Business,* July, 1965, p. 12; United States Department of Commerce, *Personal Income by States Since 1929* (Washington, D. C., United States Government Printing Office, 1956), p. 46. Additional data supplied by the New York State Department of Commerce.
** Indicates a rate higher than the nation.

displays a pattern not too dissimilar to the State and upstate.

Since certain industries grew in wages and salaries at a faster rate than did the total wage and salary income of all industry, these industries now account for a greater percentage of total "paid wages and salaries" than was previously the case. In the Region specifically, agriculture accounts for less of the total both absolutely and relatively, while services-public administration emerges as the major "growth" sector in terms of payroll disbursements. It also was a major growth industry in employment.

The divergence between regional and national growth rates in wage and salary incomes can be explained partially by the Region's lack of gain in employment. In fact, wages per employee could be increasing despite a decrease in total wage income if the number of employees is decreasing at a faster rate than wages.

123

Table C-41

Growth in Wages and Salaries Per Employee *
1964-1948

	Total	F	C	Mfg.	TPUC	WRT	FIRE	SPA
			(Per cent)					
Nation	4.1	2.8	4.5	2.7	2.5	3.8	4.5	5.3
New York	3.4	1.0	4.6**	1.4	2.8**	4.0**	4.3	5.6**
Upstate	3.5	1.2	4.3	.4	2.7**	6.3**	5.5**	5.1
Region	3.3	+	3.5	1.3	3.1**	4.1**	3.8	5.9**

* New York State Department of Labor, *Employment, Payrolls and Earnings in Establishments Covered by Unemployment Insurance: 1942-1962;* pp. 31, 33, 35, 38, 42, and 46; New York State Department of Labor, *Employment Review,* July, 1965, Tables 1 and 11; United States Bureau of the Census, *County Business Patterns 1948,* Pt. 1, Table 1a.

** Indicates a rate higher than United States.

+ A value less than 0.05.

Table C-42

Mohawk Employment and Earnings Data *
1960

	Total	AFF	C&M	Mfg.	TPUC	WRT	FIRE	SPA &NR
Employment (Unemp. Ins.)	103,662	....	4,262	59,501	5,505	21,687	4,504	8,203
Employment (Census)	170,542	9,796	8,152	62,176	8,117	25,782	5,305	51,214
Unemp. Ins. Census (Per cent)	60.8	....	52.3	95.7	67.8	84.1	84.9	16.0
Weekly Earnings	$86	....	$107	$93	$103	$68	$82	$58
New York Average Weekly Earnings	$102	....	$137	$125	$108	$119	$92	$101
Region/New York (Per cent)	84.3	....	78.1	74.4	95.4	57.1	89.1	57.4

* United States Bureau of the Census, *United States Census of Population 1960,* Vol. I, Pt. 34, Table 85; New York State Department of Labor, *Employment, Payrolls, and Earnings in Establishments Covered by Unemployment Insurance* (Albany, 1965), pp. 3, 31, 34, 35, 38, 42, and 46.

To illustrate: For the United States, while total wage and salary income increased at a 5.9 per cent growth rate and employed workers increased at a 1.8 per cent growth rate, wage and salary incomes per

employee increased at a 4.1 per cent growth rate (5.9–1.8=4.1).
The subtraction of growth rates presents the following results.[13]

As the two tables above indicate,[14] growth in employment and
growth in wage-salaries did not occur equally for each industry, and
average weekly earnings and increases in earnings per employee
tended to be below the nation's standard. Using Old Age and Survivors Insurance data for 1962, which, like unemployment data,
account only for approximately sixty per cent of all employment and
include only a small number of agricultural and government employees, one can construct differential wage rates existing between
selected manufacturing industries.

Table C-43

Average Wages Per Hour for Selected Manufactures *
1962

	Total	Textile	Apparel	Lumber; Wood	Leather	Machinery Except Electrical
Nation	$2.65	$1.80	$1.59	$1.81	$1.76	$2.96
Region	2.32	2.22**	1.42	1.85**	1.66	2.65

* United States Bureau of the Census, *County Business Patterns 1962,* Part 1, Table 1A; Part 3A, Tables 1 and 2.

** Indicates a rate higher than United States.

Only textiles and lumber-wood products of the selected regional
manufacturing industries had average hourly wage rates higher than
the national averages for firms in these same industries. When combined, these two types of manufacturing unfortunately provide less
than fifteen per cent of the Region's total manufacturing employment.

---

[13] Differences in reporting periods and data sources make it impossible to obtain exactly comparable time series data for annual wage and salary incomes and employment. Therefore, growth rates for wage and salary incomes are based on a 1948-1964 time period, and those for employment on a 1940-1960 time period.

[14] The use of the two sources of employment data, which lack complete comparability, requires a statement of warning to the reader. The results of this analysis cannot be accepted uncritically, but the authors believe that they are substantially correct, and do reflect actual influences on the Region's income.

125

Apparel, one of the few relative employment growth industries, pays below average wages and salaries.

From the foregoing analysis, it would appear that the Mohawk Region's manufacturing sector is composed of a large number of low-paying manufacturing industries, and that the firms in the Region tend to pay lower than average national rates for these industries. The average total hourly wage in the Region is thirty-three cents lower than the national average. Average wage rates for apparel and leather in the Region are not only lower than the Region's total average rate, but lower than the national rate in the same industry. Machinery, which has the highest average wage rate of the listed manufacturers for both the Region and the nation, has a low regional *vis-a-vis* national wage rate.

The Region's Economic Growth and Population Change

Economic growth is viewed in a number of different ways and measured through diverse statistical series. One commonly used series — the one used herein — compares changes in total population to changes in total income, to measured changes in per capita income. Per capita income is often viewed as the best single measure of the economic welfare of a population and its change as the best indicator of increased or decreased economic well-being.

The following graphs are constructed in such a manner as to provide information on the relationship between changes in total personal income and total population. The adjustments made for price changes provide comparisons of per capita incomes in real as well as current dollars.[15]

As the graphs indicate, the Mohawk Region had per cent changes in population and total personal income in 1948-1964 below those of New York State and upstate, while all three of these areas lagged below national averages. The Region, for the same period, had a greater lag in average change in per capita income, though it did not suffer any loss in real income; this would have been the case had

---

[15] See Harvey S. Perloff, *et. al., Regions, Resources, and Economic Growth* (Baltimore: The Johns Hopkins Press, 1960), pp. 28-33; and Edgar M. Hoover and Joseph L. Fisher, "Research in Regional Economic Growth," *Problems in the Study of Economic Growth* (New York: National Bureau of Economic Research, 1949), pp. 195-203.

Graph C-4   Economic Growth 1948-1964

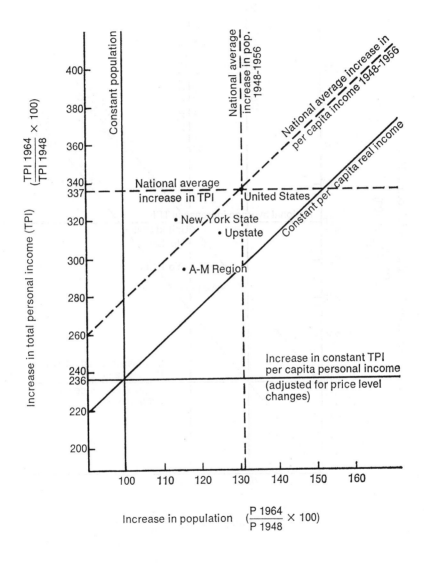

Graph C-5   Economic Growth 1948-1956

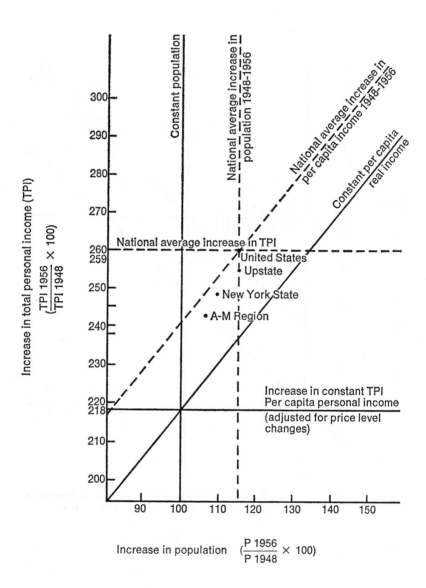

Graph C-6   Economic Growth 1957-1964

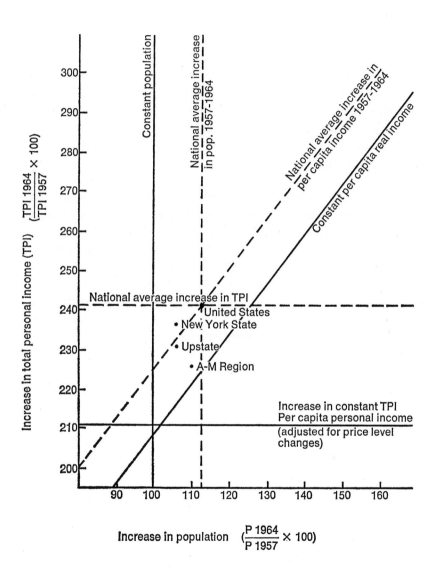

the point representing the Region fallen below the solid diagonal. Of the three New York areas, the State had the highest average per cent change in total personal income, upstate had the greatest change in total population, and the Mohawk Region lagged the other two areas. The State as a whole had a greater per cent change in per capita income than did the United States.

By disaggregating the sixteen-year period into two shorter periods, 1948-1956 and 1957-1964, a somewhat more detailed description of economic growth is presented. During one of the periods New York State surpassed the United States rates of change for per capita income. The Region had slower changes in both total and per capita incomes than did the other areas in all three periods.

As to differences occurring during the two periods, the upstate area during 1948-1956 had higher per cent changes in all three factors than did the State and the Region. During the 1957-1964 period, the State as a whole had the highest changes in total personal income and per capita income. The Region's population change was closer to that of the nation, but its personal income change was not very much greater than the price change.

The use of changes in income and population to indicate economic growth has been charactertized by a number of persons as "simple growth". What is required to present a picture of "fuller growth," it is argued, are measures of changes in structural characteristics. The data analyzed previously permit a few summary statements concerning changes in the Region's population characteristics.

Table C-44

Changes in Mohawk Region's Population and Employment 1960-1940

			Employment:	(1960)	173,023
Population:	(1960)	466,831		(1940)	151,019
	(1940)	397,905			22,004
		68,926			
			Primary:		
Sex:	(Male)	29,475	Agriculture	−7,089	
	(Female)	39,451	Forestry, Fishing	74	
		68,926	Mining	216	
			Construction	2,420	−4,379
Age:	(0-17)	55,873			
	(18-64)	−5,165	Secondary:		
	(65-)	18,216	Food and Kindred	1,132	
		68,926	Textile	−14,008	
			Apparel	3,590	
Nativity:	(Native white)	83,351	Lumber and Wood	−283	
	(Non-white)	4,271	Printing	1,225	
	(Other) Correction→	18,696	Chemicals	38	
		68,926	Electrical Machinery	11,958	
			Motor Vehicles and Parts	−172	
Settlement:	(Urban)	28,529	Other Transportation	1,096	
	(Rural Non Farm)	31,361	Misc. Mfg.	−6,777	−2,201
	(Rural Farm)	−14,562			
		68,926	Tertiary:		
			T.P.U.C.	746	
Household:	(Household)	52,051	F.I.R.E.	2,066	
	(Group Quarters)	16,875	W.R.T.	4,250	
		68,926	Medical and Professional	9,631	
			Public Administration	8,713	24,516
Labor:	(Labor Force, total)	12,036	Armed Forces	2,481	
	(Males)	1,438	Other Services	−3,371	
	(Females)	13,474			
	(Non-Labor Force, total)		Not Reported:	4,068	
	(Males)	30,913			
	(Females)	25,977			
		56,890			
		68,926	Total		22,004

131

CHAPTER 4

Commutation and Migration

Though there exists no generally accepted theory of population growth at present, it is widely agreed that population structure is strongly influenced by economic conditions. Our previous analysis indicated the changes which occurred in the population characteristics of the Mohawk Region during the 1940-1964 time period. There appears to be significant evidence that patterns of natural increase tend to change very slowly in response to shifts in economic conditions, and that more immediate changes in population characteristics are the result of changes in regional patterns of commuting and migration. In this portion of the study we are concerned with the level and patterns of commuting and migration which are displayed in the Mohawk Region.

Commutation

Data enumerating inter-county commuting patterns of persons permit partial reconciliation of employment and income statistics which are collected either on the basis of county of residence or employment. Detailed commuting information offers a bridge between these two types of employment data: residence data permit the determination of the total number of employed residents in a county; establishment data indicate the number of persons employed by firms in the county. Presented with data on the place of work of the county residents, one can determine the number of county residents employed in establishments in the same county, and how much of the economic data on income and employment composition collected on the basis of establishments is applicable to the particular county or region under study.

Reconciliation of employment data has been made for the Mohawk Region and its constituent counties, and is represented in summary form. It has been constructed from the data provided by the New York State Department of Commerce.[1] This is the first time detailed information of this type has been available for New York State, and is derived from information collected for 1960 *United States Census of Population.*

Inter-Regional Commutation

The Region had a net out-flow of 1,050 commuters in 1960. One thousand fifty more residents of the Mohawk Region were employed outside the Region than residents of other New York regions were employed within the Region.

Table D-1

Commuting of Workers for the Mohawk Region and Counties**
1960*

| | Persons Residing In Area | | |
	Net Commuters	Total Employment In Area Establishments	Per cent of Area Employment Filled by Residents
Region	— 1,050	169,400	91.9
Fulton County	— 1,900	18,250	95.9
Hamilton County	— 125	1,350	92.6
Herkimer County	— 2,000	23,500	89.4
Lewis County	— 625	7,300	95.9
Montgomery County	— 600	22,000	88.6
Oneida County	4,200	97,000	92.3
SMSA	2,200	120,500	91.7
New York State	140,000	6,740,000	98.6

* New York State Department of Commerce, *Commuting From County to County in New York State* (Albany, 1965), p. 7.

** Differences in total employment and Mohawk Region establishments are due to the original data and not compiling errors. The original data were derived from a sample.

This net figure disguises, or is the result of, a great deal of movement, since 28,700 persons were involved in the inter-regional commuting process: 13,825 into the Region and 15,875 out of the Region. This means that 8.7 per cent of the employed residents of the Mohawk Region were employed outside the Region, while at the same time, commuters from areas outside the Region constituted 8.1 per cent of those persons employed by establishments in the Mohawk Region.

[1] New York State Department of Commerce, *Commuting From County to County in New York State* (Albany: 1965).

133

Table D-2

Commuting of Workers for the Mohawk Region and Counties*

1960

	Employed Civilians	Out Commuters	Out Commuters As Per cent of Employed Civilians	In Commuters
Region	170,400	14,875	8.7	13,825
Fulton County	20,250	2,800	13.9	900
Hamilton County	1,500	225	14.9	100
Herkimer County	25,500	4,500	17.6	2,500
Lewis County	7,900	950	12.2	325
Montgomery County	22,750	3,100	13.8	2,500
Oneida County	92,500	3,300	3.6	7,500
SMSA	118,000	7,800	6.6	10,000
New York State	6,599,000	74,000	1.1	214,000

* New York State Department of Commerce, *Commuting From County to County in New York State* (Albany, 1965), p. 7.

Estimates of Net Commuting 1948-1960

Wage and salary income figures are derived for the counties of New York State on two different bases. These are (1) an estimate of total wage and salary income payed out or disbursed by establishments in the Mohawk Region and (2) an estimate of total wage and salary income received by persons residing in the Mohawk Region. The difference between these two totals is the amount of income attributable to net commuting for the Region. The differential figure thus obtained provides at least two types of information — the magnitude and importance of net commuting in the Region's total income — as well as the direction of the Region's net commuting. If a greater amount of wage and salary income is paid out by establishments in the Region than is received by residents, wage and salary income is being exported out of the Region. If the reverse is true, there is an importation of income into the area caused by net out-commuting.

Between 1950 and 1952, the Region changed from a net receiver of commuters to a net supplier of commuters to other areas, a switch from net in-commuting to net out-commuting. The peak year for net out-commuting for the Mohawk Region was 1956 when net commuters accounted for an additional 10.3 million dollars of wage and salary incomes to the Region's total personal income.

Since information concerning absolute numbers of commuters is not available before 1960, one can only estimate the impact of commuting on the total economy of the Region before this period. Rough estimates of this impact can be constructed using the available income figures. Starting with 1952, the relative importance of income earned by residents of the Region through their net out-commuting can be established. This is done by determining the portion of total wage and salary incomes of Mohawk residents attributable to net out-commuting.[2]

Table D-3

Total Wage and Salary Differentials for the Mohawk Region*

Year	Total Wage and Salary Received By Residents (000,000)	Total Wage and Salary Disbursed (000,000)	Import (000,000)	Export (000,000)	Net-Commuting
1948	$396.7	$404.7		$8.0	in
1950	404.5	407.7		3.2	in
1952	479.0	472.0	$7.7		out
1954	516.1	510.1	6.0		out
1956	585.8	575.5	10.3		out
1958	610.5	605.7	4.8		out
1960	666.4	659.8	6.6		out

* Compiled from data supplied by New York State Department of Commerce, Division of Economic Research and Statistics.

Net out-commuters contributed between 1.8 and 0.6 per cent of the total wages and salaries received by residents of the Mohawk Region. As with any net or total figure, changes may be attributable to a number of factors, for the total is the result of changes in components, and in a case such as presented here, we have little knowledge regarding which components contributed the greatest change. Gross commutation figures are available for 1960 only and consequently, comparison of change in the level and composition of net commuting cannot be made.

---

[2] The data are in current dollars; adjustment for changes in price level would not, of course, change the per cent data.

Table D-4

Per Cent of Total Resident Wage and Salary Attributable to Net Out-Commuting*

Year	Per cent
1952	1.6
1954	1.2
1956	1.8
1958	0.6
1960	1.0

* Compiled from data supplied by New York State Department of Commerce, Division of Economic Research and Statistics.

Estimates of Wage and Salary Differentials for Commuters

The availability of these gross statistics does permit certain types of analyses not possible previously. Combining the gross figures for commuting in 1960 and the data on wage and salary incomes provided above, one can attempt to provide a crude estimate of the difference in average annual wages earned by commuters out of the Region and those persons who both reside and work in the Region.

The methodology used for this analysis is presented below:

Wage and Salary Differentials Attributable to Out-Commuters, Mohawk Region, 1960

(1) Number of Employed Resident Civilians =   170,400

(2) Residents Employed Outside of Region =   14,875

(3) Residents Employed in Region =   155,525

(4) Commuters into Region =   13,825

(5) Total Employment in Region =   169,350

(6) Average Wages and Salaries Received by Employees in the Region = Total Wages and Salary Disbursements in Region ÷ Total Employed in Region = $659.8 million ÷ 169.4 = $3,895.

(7) Average Wage and Salary Received by Residents of the Region = Total Wage and Salary Received in Region ÷ Total Employed Civilians Residing in Region = $666.4 million ÷ 170.4 = $3,911.

136

(8) Total Wage and Salary Received by Residents of Region who work in Region = (3) x (6) = $605.8 million.

(9) Average Wage and Salary Received by Out-Commuters from Region= Total Wage and Salary Receipts for Region - (8) ÷ Total Out-Commuters = $666.4 - $605.8 ÷ 14,875 = $60.6 ÷ 14,875 = $4,074.

(10) Differential Wage Received by Out-Commuters = (9) - (6) = $179.

Residents of the Mohawk Region who work outside of the Region receive average annual wages and salaries which are $179 greater than those received by Mohawk residents who work in the Region.

This is, admittedly, a crude estimate, and the methodology used is subject to a great deal of refinement, but it does provide some indication of the differential in incomes between the Region's commuters and non-commuters. This analysis deals with commuters who leave the Region, and does not apply or attempt to apply, to intra-regional commuters. A great deal more sophistication must be brought to bear on the analysis of this phenomenon, including estimates of the cost of commuting. If one is willing to accept that commuters from the Mohawk Region earn higher wages and salaries — a result fully complementary to regional economic theory — than those who remain to work in the Region, a question may be raised regarding where these higher incomes are earned.

The direction and magnitude of the commuting activity centered about the Region are represented on Map D-1. This map does not attempt to portray all the inter-regional commuting which takes place between the Mohawk and other regions, but confines itself to major commuting flows. More detailed and complete statistics on commuting are presented in the discussion of inter-county commuting which follows this presentation of regional data.

The heaviest amount of inter-regional commuting takes place at the eastern and western extremities of the Region. More commuters leave the Region at its eastern boundaries than commute in. The opposite is true of the west. The usual explanation of commuting rests on employment opportunity, income differentials, and proximity. It is generally assumed that most commuting takes place towards

137

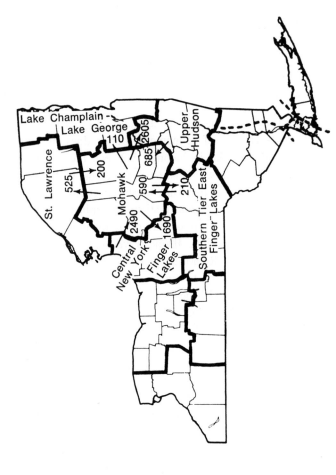

Map D - 1 Commuting Pattern of the Mohawk Region, 1960*

* New York State Department of Commerce, *Commuting From County to County in New York State* (Albany, 1965), pp. 44, 47, 48, 50, 54 and 57.

urban centers, with larger centers attracting more commuters than smaller. Gravity models have been constructed which illustrate these factors. Given such explanations, and the economic character of the Mohawk Region, it is possible to provide at least a superficial analysis of the commuting patterns affecting the Region.

The eastern portion of the Region has experienced a noticeable decline in economic activity in recent years. Wage rates in this area can be shown to be below those received in similar employment elsewhere in the State and nation. On its southeast, the Mohawk Region borders on the Upper Hudson Region generally, and the Albany-Schenectady-Troy SMSA specifically. Economic growth in the latter SMSA has been more vigorous than the growth which has taken place in the eastern portion of the Region, and persons have been moving from this slow growth area to the high growth area. The population centers in this section of the Mohawk Region, particularly Amsterdam, are close to the Albany-Schenectady-Troy SMSA, and travel to this area from the Region has been facilitated by the construction of the New York Thruway. Employment opportunities and incomes offered by this SMSA have been sufficient to offset part of the cost of commuting, and persons from the Mohawk Region are willing to travel the necessary distances to gain employment.

In the western portion of the Mohawk Region, the picture is somewhat reversed. This portion of the Region has been able to maintain higher levels of economic growth than the eastern area, and it also contains the Region's SMSA, Utica-Rome. The discussion of commuting patters affecting the counties of the Region will present a more detailed picture of the flow of commuters over the boundaries of the Mohawk Region, and it should be mentioned here that the bulk of commuting between the Central New York-Finger Lakes Region and the Mohawk Region takes place between Madison County and the southern part of Oneida County. Manufacturing plants located close to the common borders of these two counties account for much of the commuting which takes place.

Although the Utica-Rome SMSA is located in the western portion of the Mohawk Region, its growth has not been as strong as that of the Syracuse SMSA which is situated to the west of the Region. This SMSA — composed of Madison, Onondaga and Oswego Counties — attracts a large number of in-commuters who reside in the counties bordering the Mohawk Region on the west, Madison and Oswego. Of the 2,490 persons commuting into the Mohawk Region from the west, 2,100 come from Madison County. This same county sends 3,700 workers to Onondaga County.

The out-commuting of Mohawk residents to the St. Lawrence Region and Lake Champlain-Lake George Region is readily explainable. These are persons living in the northern portion of the Mohawk Region where there is little manufacturing activity and limited job opportunities. Residents of this area must seek employment elsewhere, and these choose to go out of the Region though this requires a large amount of travel.

As indicated in Table D-1 and Table D-2, five of the six counties of the Mohawk Region experienced net out-commuting in 1960. For each of these counties out-commuters constituted over ten per cent of the total employment of resident civilians. Herkimer County had the highest percentage of out-commuters with 17.6 per cent of its employed residents being employed out of the county.

Oneida County offers the only exception to this general pattern of out-commuting. It is the only county which had more workers coming into its boundaries than leaving.

In terms of relying on in-commuters to fill jobs within the county, the importance of in-commuters varied between 4.1 per cent of employment in the county of Fulton and Lewis to 11.4 per cent for Montgomery. Montgomery County filled 11.4 per cent of its jobs with non-county residents, while 13.8 per cent of its own employed civilians gained employment outside the county.

Although there is relatively little data available dealing with the commuting patterns between cities and urban places, a small amount of information is available in the *United States Census of Population of 1960,* and this is provided below.

Amsterdam's provision of over half the out-commuters from Montgomery County is not particularly surprising. This city contains 50.2 per cent of the county population, experienced a low degree of economic growth, is situated at the eastern extremity of the Region in close proximity to the Albany-Schenectady-Troy SMSA, and is located on the New York Thruway.

Map D-2 Commuting Pattern of the Counties of the Mohawk Region, 1960*

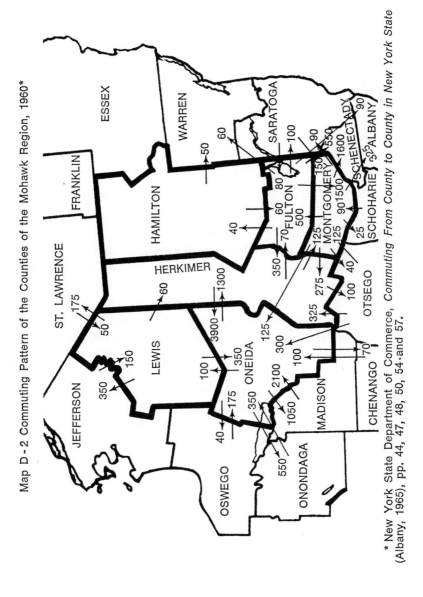

* New York State Department of Commerce, *Commuting From County to County in New York State* (Albany, 1965), pp. 44, 47, 48, 50, 54 and 57.

141

Table D-5

Commuting From Urban Places of 10,000 Persons or More*
1959

	Residents Employed	Per Cent Working in County	Per Cent Working Outside County	Per Cent Of Total County Out-Commuters	Urban Place Is Situated In the County of
Gloversville	8,505	89.3	6.6	21.1	Fulton
Johnstown	4,056	89.0	8.8	13.3	Fulton
Ilion	3,960	81.8	15.8	14.4	Herkimer
Amsterdam	11,301	81.6	15.5	56.0	Montgomery
Rome	17,569	95.2	1.3	6.4	Oneida
Utica	36,903	91.1	3.1	31.4	Oneida

* United States Bureau of the Census, *United States Census of Population 1960*, Vol. 1, Pt. 34, Table 72.

Once again using differentials in total wage and salary incomes for residents and persons employed in the counties of the Mohawk Region, it is possible to establish estimates of net commuting for the counties. The pattern of net migration varied over time, with Fulton and Herkimer Counties changing from net in-to net out-commuting between 1948 and 1950, and Montgomery County making this change between 1950 and 1956. On the basis of the data available, Hamilton County maintained an even balance of net commuting until the 1956-1960 period when out-commuting became dominant, Lewis County was a consistent net out-commuter, and Oneida County was a consistent net in-commuter. For the five net in-commuter counties, wage and salary income earned outside the county accounted for between ten and sixteen per cent of total wage and salary income of county residents.

The pattern of inter-county commuting, as indicated by Map D-2, presents a more detailed picture of regional commuting flows. The noticeable east-west split exists in intra-regional and for inter-regional commuting. Comparatively little commuting took place in a westerly direction from Hamilton, Fulton, or Montgomery Counties. These three counties either sent commuters to each other or to bordering counties on the east.

Table D-6

Total Wage and Salary Differentials For Counties*
1960-1948

	Total Wages And Salaries Received (000,000)	Total Wages And Salaries Disbursed (000,000)	Imports of Wages And Salaries (000,000)	Exports of Wages And Salaries (000,000)	Per Cent of Total Wages And Salaries Imported	Net Commuting
Fulton						
1948	$40.4	$42.1	$	$1.7		in
1950	42.9	42.8	0.1		0.2	out
1956	54.7	51.8	2.0		5.1	out
1960	67.7	58.2	9.5		14.0	out
Hamilton						
1948	3.5	3.5	0.0			
1950	2.9	2.9	0.0			
1956	3.5	3.5	0.0			
1960	5.1	4.5	0.6		11.7	out
Herkimer						
1948	58.1	61.1		3.0		in
1950	54.7	54.3	0.3		0.5	out
1956	71.9	69.3	2.6		3.6	out
1960	89.5	75.2	14.3		16.0	out
Lewis						
1948	13.0	11.7	1.3		10.0	out
1950	13.7	12.2	1.5		11.0	out
1956	19.1	17.5	1.6		9.9	out
1960	23.7	19.9	3.8		16.0	out
Montgomery						
1948	65.3	67.9		2.6		in
1950	64.6	66.4		1.8		in
1956	72.3	65.5	6.8		8.0	out
1960	76.6	68.7	7.9		10.3	out
Oneida						
1948	216.4	218.4		2.0		in
1950	225.7	228.9		3.2		in
1956	364.3	367.9		3.6		in
1960	403.8	443.4		29.6		in

* New York State Department of Commerce, *Personal Income in Counties of New York State 1963* (Albany: 1965), p. 7.

Residents of the three other counties of the Region commuted either to their western border counties or among themselves. Herkimer and Oneida Counties very much appear as a commuting unit, as one would expect for the counties of an SMSA. Additional heavy commuting which occurred in Oneida has been mentioned earlier in the discussion of the Region. While Lewis County had some commuting activity, it appears to have been a little more strongly drawn by employment opportunities offered in Jefferson and St. Lawrence Counties.

In summary, the commuting pattern of the Mohawk Region and its counties, exhibited a marked east-west flow. This applies to both inter- and intra-regional commuting. Also, where previously the Mohawk Region had imported workers and exported incomes, the reverse became the case.

Migration

The long-run movement of population as an adjustment to economic change and opportunity is population migration. Population migration, of course, takes place over longer distances than commuting, but there is an unquestionably strong relationship between these two phenomena. The causal factors for both forms of activity may be very much the same, but there is as yet little detailed data of the characteristics of commuting and migration populations available which would permit an analysis of these causal factors.

Net Migration: Counties

Since little specific data concerning migration are available, one usually is forced to fall back on derived migration estimates. Most commonly, one finds that estimates have been constructed for net migration using a residual method,[3] and this method was used in establishing the estimates of net migration.

---

[3] The Residual Method consists of the following:

$$M_o = (P_{t+o} - P_t) - \cancel{N_o}\ N_o\ (Correction)$$

Where M_o = net migration during the time period under study,
P_{t+o} = total population of the study area in final year of time period,
P_t = total population of the study area in first year of time period,
N_o = net natural increase during time period,

144

Five counties lost a portion of their potential population growth, based on natural increases, through population migration. Fulton, Hamilton, and Lewis Counties had net outflows of population which constitute the majority of their net natural increases. For Montgomery County, the outflow of population was so great that it not only offset any growth which might have resulted from natural increases, but actually caused an absolute decline in population.

Table D-7

Net Population Migration*
1960-1950

	1960-1950 Total Population Change	1960-1950 Net Natural Increase	Net Migration	Net Migration As a Per Cent of Net Natural Increase
Region	45,328	47,849	— 2,521	— 5.3
Fulton County	283	3,478	— 3,195	— 91.9
Hamilton County	162	355	— 193	— 54.4
Herkimer County	4,963	5,949	— 986	— 16.6
Lewis County	728	3,569	— 2,841	— 79.6
Montgomery County	— 2,354	4,001	— 6,355	— 158.8
Oneida County	41,546	30,497	11,049	36.2

* Derived from population data in the *United States Census of Population 1950* and *1960*; and from the *Annual Statistical Report* of the New York State Department of Health, 1950 and 1960.

The most notable change in net migration between 1950-1960 and 1940-1950 was the significant increase in out-migration from Fulton County which moved from a net receiver of population to a net supplier. The rate of net out-migration also increased greatly for Montgomery County, making it an absolute loser of population in the 1950-1960 period. Hamilton and Lewis Counties, while losing population absolutely through net out-migration between 1940-1950, changed to relative population losers in the latter period. Oneida County became a much more significant gainer in population through net migration during the latter period, 1950-1960.

Statistics on net migration reveal little more than absolute totals. One still is not permitted to make any comment concerning the composition of the migrating population. No comprehensive data

145

Table D-8

Net Population Migration*
1950-1940

	1950-1940 Total Population Change	1950-1940 Net Natural Increase	Net Migration	Net Migration As a Per Cent of Net Natural Increase
Region	23,598	29,194	− 5,596	− 19.2
Fulton County	2,424	2,284	140	6.1
Hamilton County	− 83	209	− 292	− 139.7
Herkimer County	1,880	4,227	− 2,347	− 55.5
Lewis County	− 294	2,122	− 2,416	− 113.8
Montgomery County	452	2,839	− 2,387	− 84.1
Oneida County	19,219	17,513	1,706	9.7

* Derived from data in the *United States Census of Population 1950* and *1940*; and from the *Annual Statistical Report* of the New York State Department of Health, 1950 and 1940.

dealing with the social and economic characteristics of persons who migrate are readily available. Though more attention has been given to the problems of both migration and commuting in recent years, much work still remains to be done.

Recently, statistics have become available which disaggregate net population migration for counties by both sex and age. It is now possible to examine net migration on the basis of these two population characteristics.

Table D-9 highlights the large amount of net migration which occurred among persons fifteen to twenty-nine years of age. Persons in this age group are crucially important for family and employment growth. For example, previous discussion concerning the age and sex composition of the population of the Mohawk Region indicated a relative shortage of males eighteen to sixty-four years of age. A partial explanation of this scarcity seems apparent from the figures; *i.e.* Montgomery County lost through migration 38.4 per cent of its males twenty to twenty-four years of age, and 25 per cent of its males twenty-five to twenty-nine years of age. Female rates, though high, were not as great as the rates for males. This same pattern, to a greater or lesser degree, exists for each county except Oneida. Based on common assumptions, five counties lost young males who were

Table D-9

Net Migration by Age and Sex*
1960-1950

	15-19 Male	Female	20-24 Male	Female	25-29 Male	Female
	(Per Cent)		(Per Cent)		(Per Cent)	
Fulton	— 12.8	— 12.8	— 30.0	— 21.2	— 22.9	— 17.5
Hamilton	— 6.6	— 7.7	— 47.6	— 28.4	— 25.5	— 29.8
Herkimer	— 9.8	— 8.7	— 25.5	— 15.7	— 5.8	— 2.1
Lewis	— 21.2	— 18.0	— 21.8	— 33.4	— 28.1	— 21.6
Montgomery	— 19.7	— 15.1	— 38.4	— 25.0	— 25.0	— 16.0
Oneida	.6	— .4	— 2.0	6.5	14.3	13.0

* Derived from data in United States Department of Agriculture, *Net Migration of the Population, 1950-1960, By Age, Sex, and Color,* Vol. 1., Pt. 1 (Washington, D.C.: United States Government Printing Office, 1965).

either just entering or had just entered into the more physically productive period of their economic life. The counties, therefore, suffered a decline in income potential. It also must be assumed that it was the lack of economic opportunity in the home county compared to economic advantages of other areas which caused this movement of younger persons.

The commonly used residual technique for estimating net migration contains a number of weaknesses, the major one of which stems from the fact that one is working with net change: the residual change. A net figure may in fact hide a great deal of activity or population movement which tend to cancel each other. Net figures do not provide knowledge of the number of persons migrating-in or of the number migrating-out of an area. It is not possible to discuss the flow of population movement, its origins or destinations, or even the gross figures for movement to and from an area. All that can be said using net figures is that a certain residual portion of the population either has entered or left a particular area.

Nativity and residence data provided in the *United States Census of Population* allow the construction of gross migration estimates for 1950-1960. Gross and net figures for population migration of the six counties are presented here, but the data available do not allow a similar analysis of the net migration figure for the Mohawk Region as a total. It is not possible, from the information provided, to separate migrations between counties into inter- or intra-regional migrations.

Gross Migration: Counties

Table D-10 presents evidence of the amount of migration or population movement which occurred for the counties. Based on net migration figures alone, one could only say that a net of 986 persons actually migrated from Herkimer County, with no idea of how much activity the movement of these 986 persons actually represented. With the data given below, it can be seen that the net figure was the result of the movement of 28,690 persons, 13,852 out and 14,838 in. The same type of analysis of population migration is possible for each of the counties. Given the population bases of the counties in 1950, it is quite apparent that migration played an extremely important role in the composition of their populations and economies.

Table D-10

Gross Population Migration*
1960-1950

	1960-1950 Population Increase	1960-1950 Net Natural Increase	In	—	Migration Out =	Net
Fulton	293	3,478	6,954	—	10,149 =	− 3,195
Hamilton	162	355	980	—	1,173 =	− 193
Herkimer	4,963	5,949	13,852	—	14,838 =	− 986
Lewis	728	3,569	4,212	—	7,053 =	− 2,841
Montgomery	− 2,354	4,001	8,418	—	14,773 =	− 6,355
Oneida	41,546	30,497	61,180	—	50,131 =	11,049
SMSA	46,509	36,466	75,032	—	64,196 =	10,063

* Derived from population data in the *United States Population Census 1950* and *1960*; and vital statistics presented in the New York State Department of Health *Annual Statistical Report*, 1960 and 1950.

After having moved this one step closer to a detailed picture of population migration, a very important factor is still missing. One still is not able to indicate the directions of these migration flows, or which directions future migrations might take. Again much more information must be made available before such patterns of migration are clearly discernible. The *United States Census of Population* for 1960 has provided more information on previous residence and on nativity than any of the previous censuses, and it is possible, using certain assumptions, to establish in a general fashion where persons have migrated from.

148

Specifically, assuming that the migration pattern which existed between 1955 and 1960 existed during the entire 1950-1960 period, one can establish the following concerning the migrants into the six counties of the Mohawk Region.

Table D-11

Previous Place of Residence of Migrants into the Counties of the Mohawk Region*
1960-1950

	Resided in Different County; Same State	Resided Abroad or Different State
Fulton County	5,010	1,944
Hamilton County	778	202
Herkimer County	9,932	3,920
Lewis County	3,034	1,178
Montgomery County	6,204	2,214
Oneida County	21,990	29,190

* United States Bureau of the Census, *United States Census of Population 1960*, Vol. 1, Pt. 34, Table 82.

Using these rough estimates as a base, each county except Oneida, received the greatest portion of its in-migrants — roughly seventy-five per cent — from within the State. For Oneida, intra-state migration accounted for approximately fifty-three per cent of the in-migrants. Similar statistics for the counties out-migrants are not readily available, and so no construct of this type can be established.

Intra-state migration accounts for the major portion of migrants into all the counties of the Mohawk Region. Can one assume that the same is true for the out-migrants for each of the counties? Based on introspection and a small amount of data, the answer appears to be affirmative. Persons migrating from Mohawk Region Counties tend to migrate within the State of New York, rather than outside the State.

Until recently, there has been only spotty information concerning intra-state population migration and this dealt with a few selected areas rather than the entire State. As a result of the increasing interest being shown in questions concerning migration, the United States Census Bureau has been attempting to provide more data on population movements within the United States and its geographic areas. Previous interest has centered on international migrations, but now with the flow of international migration into the United States slowed down, interest is being turned toward internal migration patterns.

Inter-County Migration

Recent Census publications provide enough data to establish a picture of the patterns of migration taking place within state boundaries and between State Economic Areas (SEA's).[4] This information covers the period 1955-1960. New York State has been disaggregated into SEA's and population migration between these areas has been recorded.

Five counties of the Mohawk Region have been included into two separate SEA's, and so it is possible to discern the pattern of intrastate migration displayed by these Areas. Fulton, Hamilton, and Montgomery Counties form one SEA (Area 5), Oneida and Herkimer another (Area D). It is impossible to establish the migration pattern for Lewis County, which has been included with five other counties into a single SEA.

Maps D-3 through D-6 indicate the patterns of migration which took place between 1955 and 1960 for five of the Region's counties.

For Hamilton, Fulton, and Montgomery counties combined, the total number of persons migrating out between 1955 and 1960 was 7,257. Migrants into the area numbered some 4,334, constituting a net loss of 2,923 persons. These were persons who were five years old and older in 1960. Of the out-migrants, 59.6 per cent moved to economic areas adjacent to the one they had just left. Twenty-eight per cent moved into the Albany-Schenectady area and 16 per cent into Oneida-Herkimer. Accepting that the State Economic Areas designated by the letters A through G represent SMSA's, 73.6 per cent of the migrants from Area 5 moved to SMSA's. The large portion of these movers — 38.6 per cent — went to the Albany-Schenectady-Troy SMSA.

---

[4] State Economic Areas (SEA's) are relatively homogeneous subdivisions of the states. They are composed of single counties or groups of counties which have similar economic and social characteristics. See: United States Bureau of the Census, *United States Census of Population 1960, Mobility for States and State Economic Areas* (Washington, D. C.: United States Government Printing Office, 1963).

150

Map D - 3 Migration Out of Hamilton, Fulton, and Montgomery Counties, 1955 - 1960*

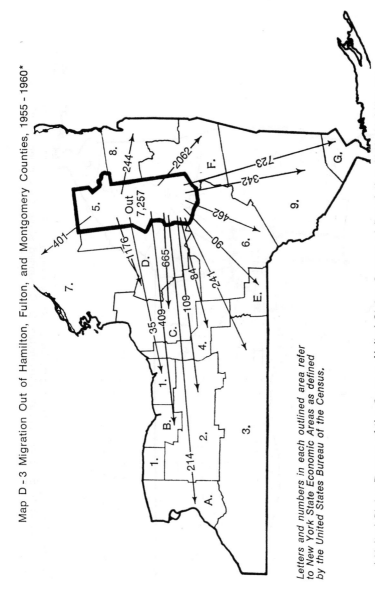

Letters and numbers in each outlined area refer to New York State Economic Areas as defined by the United States Bureau of the Census.

* United States Bureau of the Census, *United States Census of Population 1960, Mobility for States and State Economic Areas* (Washington, D. C.: United States Government Printing Office, 1963), pp. 186 - 187.

Map D - 4 Migration Out of Herkimer and Oneida Counties, 1955 - 1960*

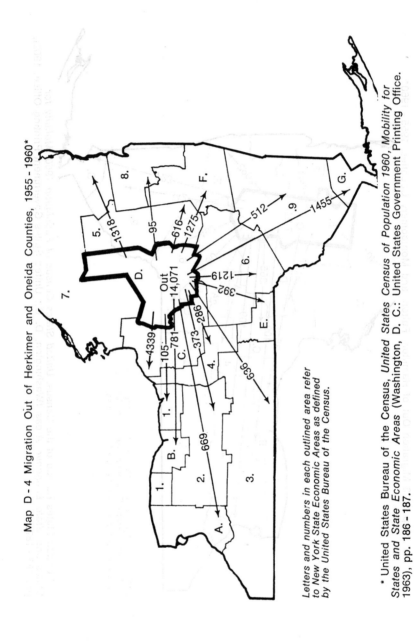

Letters and numbers in each outlined area refer
to New York State Economic Areas as defined
by the United States Bureau of the Census.

* United States Bureau of the Census, United States Census of Population 1960, Mobility for
States and State Economic Areas (Washington, D. C.: United States Government Printing Office.
1963), pp. 186 - 187.

Map D - 5 Migration Into Hamilton, Fulton, and Montgomery Counties, 1955 - 1960*

Letters and numbers in each outlined area refer to New York State Economic Areas as defined by the United States Bureau of the Census.

* United States Bureau of the Census, *United States Census of Population 1960, Mobility for States and State Economic Areas* (Washington, D. C.: United States Government Printing Office. 1963), pp. 186 - 187.

153

Map D-6 Migration Into Herkimer and Oneida Counties, 1955-1960*

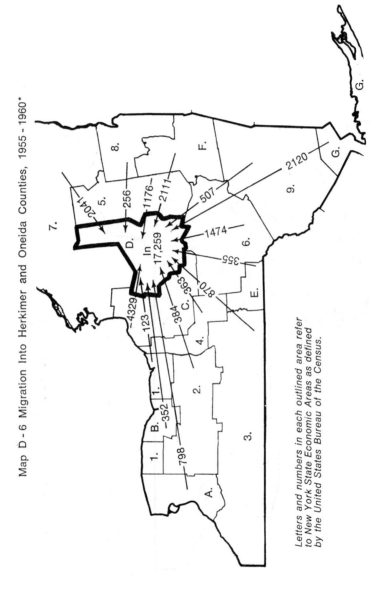

Letters and numbers in each outlined area refer
to New York State Economic Areas as defined
by the United States Bureau of the Census.

* United States Bureau of the Census, *United States Census of Population 1960, Mobility for States and State Economic Areas* (Washington, D. C.: United States Government Printing Office, 1963), pp. 186 - 187.

154

Of the 4,334 migrants into Area 5, 2,958 — 68.3 per cent — come from adjacent Herkimer County. Of the total in-migrants, approximately seventy-three per cent came from the seven SMSA's of the State. This last figure may be somewhat misleading, for if one excludes migrants from the Albany-Schenectady-Troy SMSA, Area 5 received 36 per cent of its in-migrants from SMSA's. The migration from Albany-Schenectady-Troy SMSA is somewhat of a special case. Its proximity to Montgomery County appears to be turning a portion of this County into a residential area of Schenectady. This is borne out by the figures on commuting.

There was a net in-migration of 3,178 persons, 17,259 in and 14,071 out for the Oneida-Herkimer Area — the Utica-Rome SMSA. Only fifty-two per cent of the in-migrants to Area D came from adjacent SEA's. Forty-seven per cent of all in-migrants came from other New York State SMSA's, and the bulk of these persons coming from SMSA's came from the Syracuse Area — fifty-three per cent.

Of the persons moving out of Area D, fifty-three per cent moved to adjacent Areas, almost the same per cent as those moving in, and seventy-three per cent moved to SMSA's. Some thirty per cent of all out-migrants went to the Syracuse Area which accounted for forty-nine per cent of the out-migrants who moved into State SMSA's. The heavy cross migration between Area D and Area C suggests that these Areas eventually may be conjoined. Albany received only nine per cent of out-migrants from the Herkimer-Oneida Area, while New York City received ten per cent, its attraction being a slight bit stronger than the Albany Area's.

Something now might be said about the relationships between commuting and migration for these five counties. Although the present data do not permit definitive statements on this score, it would appear that these two phenomena are closely linked and the patterns of migration and the patterns of commuting are very much the same, both in direction and in intensity. The attraction of the near-by SMSA's clearly is displayed in both the commuting and migration patterns presented by these areas, a focus for the majority of population movement between the counties. Albany-Schenectady-Troy and Syracuse SMSA's provided a large portion of the Mohawk Region's in-commuters and in-migrants, and they received a significant amount of out-commuters and out-migrants.

Gross Migration: Urban Places

Using the same techniques as described previously, it is possible to estimate the gross migration rates for all Urban Places of 10,000 persons or more within the Mohawk Region. Little analysis will be made of these population movements, for since these Urban Places constitute the population centers for their respective counties, the discussion on county migration applies here.

Table D-12

Gross Migration For Urban Places of 10,000 or More* 1960-1950

	1960-1950 Population Increase	1960-1950 Net Natural Increase	In	—	Migration Out =	Net
Gloversville	− 1,893	1,501	2,494	—	5,886 =	− 3,394
Johnstown	− 433	465	1,330	—	2,329 =	− 998
Ilion	836	752	1,906	—	1,922 =	84
Amsterdam	− 3,468	1,832	2,928	—	8,228 =	− 5,300
Rome	9,964	8,202	11,006	—	9,244 =	1,762
Utica	− 1,121	9,908	16,366	—	27,395 =	− 11,029
SMSA	46,509	36,446	75,032	—	64,969 =	10,063

* Derived from population data in the *United States Census of Population 1950* and *1960*; and vital statisics data from the New York State Department of Health *Annual Statistical Report,* 1950 and 1960.

Only two of the Region's major urban areas — Ilion and Rome — had positive net in-migration between 1950 and 1960. The other four areas had out-migrations which more than equalled net natural increases, and had net losses of persons. Rome, one of the areas to have an increase in population, required 11,000 in-migrants to offset its loss of 9,244 persons through migration. Thus, even those areas which had positive population growth 1950-1960, had a large amount of out-migration.

Data provided by the *United States Census of Population* permit one to establish the point of origin of the in-migrants to these same urban places, but here again, these data permit only the most general designation of place of origin.

Table D-13

Place of Origin of In-Migrants*
1960-1950

	Different County Same State	Different State And Abroad
Gloversville	1,666	828
Johnstown	932	398
Ilion	1,146	760
Amsterdam	1,898	1,030
Rome	4,646	6,360
Utica	9,638	6,728

* United States Bureau of the Census, *Census of Population 1960*, Vol. 1, Pt. 34, Table 72.

Each of the urban places, except Rome, received more of its in-migrants from within New York State than from outside the State or abroad. Johnstown attracted only one-quarter of its in-migrants from outside the State. The figure for Rome reflects the inflow of the large military base which is situated there.

CHAPTER 5

Economic Welfare in the Mohawk Region

Chapter 1 contained a discussion of the perspective of this study: an analysis of the lagged economic development of the six-county Mohawk Region. Questions were raised as to whether the registered increase in per capita income differentials between the Region and the nation would be sustained after examination of the composition of the Region. The changing composition of the nation also was included in the analysis. From this perspective, testable hypotheses were developed. This chapter sequentially examines each hypothesis and briefly comments on the implications of the results.

The Changing Level of Income

Though there is no way to provide an explicit answer to the question of what is the standard increase in per capita income for a region given simultaneous changes in its employment, wages, non-wage incomes, population, and other interdependent variables, indicative data can be summoned and a tentative conclusion formulated.

Between 1948 and 1964, wages and salaries per employee — summed by industry — increased at a 1.6 per cent average annual rate while those in the nation increased at a 2.4 per cent rate. Total income per capita in the Region increased at a lesser rate than it did in the nation. Non-wage income per capita increased at a somewhat more rapid rate in the Region than in the nation, but not enough to offset the limited performance of wages and salaries per employee. The data in Table E-1 are not fully comparable because the wages and salaries data are those for establishments located in the Region while the remainder of the data pertains to the residents of the Region. It is clear that the income growth in the Region was more limited than in the nation. This generalization is not altered seriously when wages and salaries per employee are compared by industry for

Table E-1

Growth Rates in Adjusted Income in the Mohawk Region*
1964-1948

	Total Income Per Capita (Per Cent)	Wages and Salaries Per Employee (Per Cent)	Non-Wage Income Per Capita (Per Cent)
Region	1.0	1.6	1.7
Nation	1.8	2.4	1.5

* Data are adjusted for changes in the price level: 1963=100.0 using the GNP deflator. Total income per capita data are derived from New York State Department of Commerce, *Personal Income in Counties of New York State 1964* (Albany, 1966), p. 2; and *Survey of Current Business,* April, 1966, p. 11. Wages and salaries data are derived from the United States Bureau of the Census, *County Business Patterns, 1964, United States Summary,* Tables 1G and 4A; and the United States Department of Commerce, *County Business Patterns, 1948, United States Summary,* Tables 1 and 4. Non-wage and salary data are derived from United States Department of Commerce, *Personal Income by States Since 1929* (Washington, D. C., 1956), Tables 4 and 13; and New York State Department of Commerce, unpublished data.

the Region and the nation. That is, given the industrial composition of the Region in 1948 and the changing composition of the nation between 1948 and 1964, the Region could have increased its wages per employee more rapidly than did the nation in several industries but have registered a lower overall rate of increase because of the differences in composition of industry beween the Region and the nation. But this is only partly fact; three of the six industries — transportation-public utilities-communications, wholesale-retail trade, and services-public administration — did register increases in wages-salaries per employee greater than did the nation by about 0.6 per cent each — 110 per cent increase over the 1948 base for the sixteen-year change.

Thus the data is probably sufficient to accept the hypothesis: lagged income growth in the Mohawk Region did exist between 1948 and 1964.

Productivity

Productivity can be approximated by measuring the change in value added and comparing it to the change in employment. The data which is readily available permit such computations for manufacturers in the Mohawk Region. The data in Table E-2 indicate that overall there was very little difference between the nation and

159

the Region in increases in productivity. Disaggregating to two-digit industries indicates productivity increases as large as 19.5 per cent and as low as -.7 per cent. The separate industry changes indicate that specialization may be occurring in the manufacture of food and kindred, apparel, leather, and furniture and fixtures. That is, the differentials from the national average increases in each of these industries indicate in a crude way the comparative advantage for the Region. This focus is really more complementary to projections than analysis, however, and is beyond the scope of this study. In total, the manufacturers in the Region did increase their productivity at about the same rate as did all manufacturers in the nation.

Table E-2

Productivity Increases for Manufacturing in the Mohawk Region*
1963, 1958, 1947

	Region (Per Cent)	U.S. (Per Cent)	Difference (Per Cent)
1963-1947			
All Manufacturers	5.3	4.9	.4
1963-1958			
Food and Kindred	19.5	4.4	15.1
Textile Mill	4.8	4.7	.1
Apparel and Related	6.7	3.3	3.4
Lumber and Wood	2.5	4.6	− 2.1
Furniture and Fixtures	10.2	3.2	7.0
Paper and Related	− .7	3.3	4.0
Printing and Publishing	2.5	3.9	− 1.4
Leather	7.0	2.6	4.4
Primary Metals	4.7	3.9	.8
Fabricated Metals	1.4	3.5	− 2.1
Transportation Equipment	10.4	6.5	3.9
Total	5.6	5.1	.5

* United States data are taken from United States Bureau of the Census, *United States Census of Manufacturers 1963, Preliminary Report: General Statistics for Industry Groups and Industries,* Table 1; Regional data are taken from United States Bureau of the Census, *United States Census of Manufacturers 1963, Area Statistics: New York,* Table 7.

Value Added and Employment

Data on value added and employment are contained in Table E-3. The data indicate that the earlier formed expectation can be accepted. Value added did increase while employment in manufacturing in the Region decreased.

Again, the totals hide an extraordinary amount of change in composition. Food and kindred products increased in value added at a 17.6 per cent rate while fabricated metal products decreased at a 3.5 per cent rate. Seven of the eleven manufacturing industries which

Table E-3

Value Added and Employment for Manufacturing in the Mohawk Region*
1963, 1958, 1947

	Growth Rate of Employment (Per Cent)		Growth Rate of Value Added (Per Cent)	
	Region	Nation	Region	Nation
1963-1947				
All Manufacturers	− 2.0	1.1	3.3	6.1
1963-1958				
Food and Kindred	− 1.9	− .6	17.6	3.8
Textile Mill	− 7.3	− .8	− 2.5	3.9
Apparel and Related	4.5	1.3	11.2	4.6
Lumber and Wood	− 3.7	− .6	− 1.2	4.0
Furniture and Fixtures	− 14.3	1.3	− 4.1	4.5
Paper and Related	2.8	1.1	2.1	4.4
Printing and Publishing	1.1	.9	3.6	4.8
Leather	1.8	− 1.1	8.8	1.5
Primary Metals	− 3.3	.5	1.4	4.4
Fabricated Metals	− 4.9	.3	− 3.5	3.8
Transportation Equip.	− 4.5	.4	5.9	6.9
Total	− 0.9	1.1	3.9	5.2

* 1947 data are from United States Bureau of the Census, *United States Census of Manufacturers 1947*, Vol. III, Tables 2 and 7; and Vol. I, Table 3. 1958 data are from United States Bureau of the Census, *United States Census of Manufacturers 1958*, Vol. III, Table 7, and Vol. I, Table 3. 1963 data are from United States Bureau of the Census, *United States Census of Manufacturers, 1963*, Vol. II, Table 7, and *Preliminary Report: General Statistics for Industry Group and Industries*, Table 1.

are reported for the Region did decrease their employment; only apparel increased employment at a much more rapid rate than did the nationwide industry — 4.5 per cent minus 1.3 per cent for a 3.2 per cent differential. Regional differentials in value added from the national manufacturing industries were most prominent in: food and kindred — differential of 13.4 per cent; apparel — differential of 6.6 per cent; and leather — differential of 7.4 per cent.

Not all of the Region's employment is in manufacturing, but data on value added in non-manufacturing are not readily available. Table E-4 indicates the changes in composition of employment in the Region. The base for computing the standards is changes in composition of national employment.

Table E-4

Employment Changes in the Mohawk Region*
1960-1940

| Industries** | Total Mohawk Region Employment | | Actual Change 1960-1940 | Change Expected on the Basis of the National Standard |
	1940	1960		
Primary	22,249	17,870	− 4,379	− 3,834
Secondary	64,378	62,177	− 2,201	24,009
Tertiary	62,068	86,584	24,516	36,790
Not Reported	2,324	6,392	4,068	6,045
Total	151,019	173,023	22,004	63,010

* United States Department of Commerce, *Growth Patterns in Employment by County*, 1940-1950 and 1950-1960, Vol. II (Washington, D.C.: 1965), Tables 1, 3, and 7.

** See Table C-44 for definitions of the industry classes.

Though the above table does not permit statements concerning value added changes, it does indicate that employment increases in the Region were but thirty-four per cent of the standard. The standard is the per cent increases in the industries in the nation multiplied times the 1940 employment in the industry in the Region and then summed across the industries to derive the standard totals.

In sum, the measurable value added and employment increases in the Mohawk Region between 1940 and 1963 were small relative to the nation.

Migration

Migration from the Mohawk Region was large; gross out-migration from the Region was 98,117 and gross in-migration was 95,596 for a net out-migration of 2,521 between 1950 and 1960. As Table D-10 indicates the net migration rates for both males and females fifteen to twenty-nine years of age were negative and ranged from two per cent to forty-seven per cent. There is some indication that the out-migration has not only been of the young but also the educated; *i.e.,* the Mohawk Region increased the per cent of persons twenty-five years of age and older without any schooling, while the State, upstate area, and nation per cents either decreased or remained unchanged during the 1950-1960 period.

Table E-5

Net Shift in Wages and Salaries From Commutation*
1964-1948

	Net Shift in Wages and Salaries from Commutation (000,000)
Fulton County	$11.2
Hamilton County	.6
Herkimer County	17.3
Lewis County	2.5
Montgomery County	10.5
Oneida County	− 27.6
Total	$14.5

* New York State Department of Commerce, *Personal Income in Counties of New York State 1964* (Albany, 1966), pp. 2-3.

Commutation

While the per cent of total residents' wages-salaries derived from net out-commutation decreased from 1.6 per cent to 1.5 per cent between 1952 and 1964, this total does not indicate the pattern of commuting behavior.

Table E-5 provides the basis for the statement that net gains from out-commutation have increased sizeably for each of the counties of the Region with the exception of Oneida. Thus the Region has changed from a net importer to a net exporter of wage and salary workers with a net gain from this trade of $14,500,000.

Table E-6

Changes in the Characteristics of the Population in the
Mohawk Region*
1960-1940

	Region	Nation	Differential
Total Change	68,926	46.795 millions	
Age			
0-17	81.1%	50.0%	31.1%
18-64	−7.5	20.0	−27.5
65 and over	26.4	30.0	−3.6
Sex			
Male	42.8%	45.3%	−2.5%
Female	57.2	54.7	2.5
Nativity			
Native White	120.9%	91.4%	29.5%
Foreign Born White	−27.1	−4.5	−22.6
Non-White	6.2	13.1	−6.9
Household Relationship			
Household Population	75.5%	101.4%	−25.9%
Persons in Group Quarters	24.5	−1.4	25.9
Labor Force Status			
Labor Force			
Males	−2.0%	15.3%	−17.3%
Females	19.5	22.0	−2.5
Total	17.5	37.3	−19.8
Non-Labor Force			
Males	44.8%	30.0%	14.8%
Females	37.7	32.7	5.0
Total	82.5	62.7	19.8
Location of Residence (1950-1960)			
Urban	62.9%	101.6%	−38.7%
Rural-Non Farm	69.2	32.6	36.6
Rural Farm	−32.1	−34.2	2.1

* Compiled from data presented in previous portions of this study.

Demographic Characteristics

Between 1940 and 1960 the Region's population changed in characteristics as did the population in the nation. Table E-6 indicates the compositional changes in age, sex, nativity, household relationship, labor force status, and location of residence.

Contrary to previously formed expectations, neither the old nor the non-white had a positive differential change relative to the nation, though the youthful, non-employed, and rural-non-farm or scattered population did have sizeable positive differentials. That women did enter the labor force in increasing numbers certainly is sustained by the data. Compared to males in the Region, the differential was 21.5 per cent — 19.5 per cent plus 2.0 per cent for males — but compared to the per cent increase in female labor force in the nation, the Region had a negative differential.

Types of Income

Table E-1 indicates that non-wage-salary income per capita increased in the Region faster than it did in the nation and faster than did total per capita income in the Region. Thus non-wage-salary income must be increasing as a percentage of total income. Table E-7 indicates the per cent changes in types of income for the Mohawk Region. Again, there has been a change in the composition of income in the Mohawk Region.

Table E-7

Total Income (Unadjusted) Changes by Type in the Mohawk Region*
1964-1948

	Average Annual Rates of Change (Per Cent)		
	Region	Nation	Differential
Total Personal Income	4.2	5.5	— 1.3
Wages and Salaries	4.1	5.8	— 1.7
Property	5.5	7.1	— 1.6
Farm	— .9	— 1.8	.9
Business and Professional	2.3	3.5	— 1.2
Other	5.7	8.1	— 2.4

* Compiled from data presented previously.

Capital, Profits, and Rates of Return

Table E-8 indicates the absolute size, change, and per cent changes for gross proprietary income — value added minus payroll — and capital expenditures for the Region's manufacturers. As indicated, gross proprietary income (GPI) and capital expenditures did increase at a lesser rate in the Region than in the nation, with the exception of capital expenditures in the 1954-1958 period.

Table E-8

Gross Proprietary Income and Capital Expenditures in the Mohawk Region*
1963, 1958, 1954

| | GPI | | | Capital | | |
	1954	1958	1963	1954	1958	1963
Region (000)	$218,982	$212,458	$296,217	$14,980	$22,457	$22,095
Intercensal Change	$6,524		$83,759		$7,477	$— 362
Intercensal Per Cent Change		— 3%	39%		50%	— 2%
Nation (000,000)	$53,919	$63,174	$92,197	$7,818	$9,076	$11,397
Intercensal Change	$9,255		$29,023		$1,258	$2,321
Intercensal Per Cent Change		17%	46%		16%	26%

* 1947 data are from United States Bureau of the Census, *United States Census of Manufacturers 1947,* Vol. III, Tables 2 and 7; and Vol. I, Table 3. 1958 data are from United States Bureau of the Census, *United States Census of Manufacturers 1958,* Vol. III, Table 7, and Vol. I, Table 3. 1963 data are from United States Bureau of the Census, *United States Census of Manufacturers 1963,* Vol. II, Table 7, and *Preliminary Report: General Statistics for Industry Group and Industries,* Table 1.

Table E-9 presents the increases in the rate of return to manufacturers in the Mohawk Region. Unlike Table E-8, the rates of returns are computed rates which indicate the profitability of investments in the separate industries in the Region. For a variety of reasons, these rates are only indications of the true profit rate. The formula used for the computation is:

Rate of Return = Change in GPI/Average Capital Expenditures. For example, the change in GPI in food and kindred products is the GPI for 1963 minus the GPI for 1958; the average capital expenditures in food and kindred products is the capital expenditures in 1963 plus the capital expenditures in 1958 divided by two. The change in GPI approximates a measure of change in gross profits; the

166

average capital expenditures approximate a measure of an investment rate. The former divided by the latter provides an approximate measure of the marginal rate of return on investment.

Table E-8 indicates a decrease in absolute level of capital expenditures in the Mohawk Region, 1958-1963, while Table E-9 indicates that the capital that was invested had a positive rate of return which was also quite high *vis-a-vis* the national rate of return for certain industries. Food and kindred, apparel and related, leather, and transportation equipment each had positive differential rates of return.

Table E-9

Increases in Rate of Return to Manufacturers in the Mohawk Region*
1963, 1958, 1954

	Region (Per Cent)	Nation (Per Cent)	Differential (Per Cent)
1963-1954			
All Manufacturers	4.05	3.80	.25
1963-1958			
Food and Kindred	16.55	2.90	13.65
Textile	− .38	2.75	− 3.13
Apparel and Related	39.95	9.23	30.72
Lumber and Wood	− .46	1.46	− 1.92
Furniture and Fixtures	− 12.81	3.97	− 16.78
Paper and Related	− .44	1.45	− 1.89
Printing and Publishing	2.71	3.48	− .77
Leather	13.78	2.99	10.79
Primary Metals	.99	1.37	− .38
Fabricated Metal	− 4.17	2.73	− 6.90
Transportation Equip.	16.17	6.09	10.08
Total	3.76	2.41	1.35

* 1947 data are from United States Bureau of the Census, *United States Census of Manufacturers 1947*, Vol. III, Tables 2 and 7; and Vol. I, Table 3. 1958 data are from United States Bureau of the Census, *United States Census of Manufacturers 1958*, Vol. III, Table 7, and Vol. I, Table 3. 1963 data are from United States Bureau of the Census, *United States Census of Manufacturers 1963*, Vol. II, Table 7, and *Preliminary Report: General Statistics for Industry Group and Industries,* Table 1. Gross proprietary income, as derived, includes depreciation, interest, rent, taxes, and other purchased business services. Capital expenditures includes expenditures made during the year for permanent additions that were chargeable to fixed asset accounts of establishments and include new additions, structures, major alterations and improvements, capitalized repairs, and new machinery and equipment.

The juxtaposition of Tables E-3 and E-9 provides some interesting insights. For each industry named above except transportation equipment, value added also had a high and postive differential with the nation. In employment, only apparel and leather had positive differentials. That is, the four industries which had differential marginal rates of return on capital investment also tended to have positive differentials on value added but not necessarily on employment. Or, two of the industries are increasing employment, value added, and profit rates, while the other two are gaining value added and profits but not employment. But Table E-2 indicates that the latter two industries, food and kindred products and transportation equipment products, had the two highest increases in productivity in the Region. Thus, productivity gains are occurring at the expense of total employment in two industries — food and kindred, and transportation equipment — but three of these differential marginal rate of return industries have increasing value added *vis-a-vis* the nation; *i.e.,* they are gaining increasing shares of the market. The fourth industry, transportation equipment, is not gaining an increasing share of the market — value added growth rate is less in the Region than in the nation— but the market itself is expanding relative to all manufactured products — 6.9 per cent in the nation for transportation equipment vs. an overall average increase for manufactured products of 5.2 per cent.

Distribution of Income

The distribution of income among families in the Region between 1950 and 1960 did become more equal; the average interdecile index for the six counties in 1950 measured .7643 and in 1960 measured .6729 for a decline of .0914 or fourteen per cent. The same pattern was exhibited for each of the six counties in the Region.

In comparison with other regions of New York, an eight-county region centered on Rochester had a decrease from .7680 to .6936; a five-county region centered on Syracuse had a decrease from .7829 to .6909; and a five-county region centered on Buffalo had a decrease from .7371 to .6743. Thus each of these somewhat comparable regions had similar directions of change; they also had similar absolute changes in the interdecile index and percentage changes.

In sum, the previously formed expectation — that the distribution of family income in the Region would not have decreased as much

168

as it did in comparable regions — must be held in abeyance until further examination of the data is possible. There is no clear pattern established from the available computations.

Summary

While the composition of industry and population in both the nation and the Region has registered changes in the period of analysis, there is sufficient evidence to sustain an affirmative answer to the question, "Did the economic welfare of the residents in the Mohawk Region decline relative to that in the nation?".

The reasons for the relative decline in economic welfare for the Region's population involve the composition of the industry and population and changes in the nation. The Region's employment was wed to certain industries which did not increase in relative employment in the nation and declined in absolute totals in the Region. Whether these industries, such as textiles and lumber, could have increased the level of employment in the Region with more vigorous cooperation between the public and private decision-makers is a moot point.

Alternatively, several new concentrations of employment are developing in the Region: food products, apparel, transportation equipment, and others. Thus the Region has adapted to change which it has been partner to by developing new partnerships. Whether these adaptations will provide for increasing levels of welfare *vis-a-vis* the nation is an important question but one which public policy can help decide. The private decision-makers will certainly be involved in planning future changes in income for the Region; whether the public decision-makers will take on an active part in this planning is up to the state and local governments involved.

169

Index